SHERWOOD CARTHEN
WITH PHIL SOMMERVILLE

SOUL'D
OUT

DECIDE TO BE
SIGNIFICANT

faithALIVE 365
Living God's Best Every Day

Soul'd Out: Decide to be Significant

ISBN: 978-0-9815531-1-5

Printed in the United States of America

Rocklin, California

To Anthony and Siobhan, my children, and the six grandchildren
you have blessed me with. Both you and your families have
grown me in ways that make me want to be the best I can be. May
you always experience my love.

And to Greg, Evan, Stacey, and Tima—you were the first to call
me dad way back when I had no clue what I was doing.
Thanks for allowing me to practice on you what would eventually
be given to the masses.

And finally, to Benjamin, my first grandson—you have taught me
to never underestimate the power of God. Our relationship means
more to me than you will ever know. Because of you I am a better
person, and hopefully a better Papa.

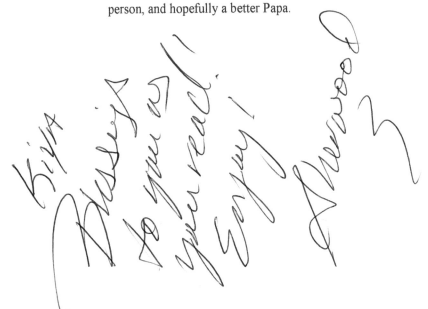

Acknowledgments

I would like to say thanks to Phil Sommerville and his wife, Linda, for their friendship and partnership on this book project. You opened up your home, dispensed treats, and allowed me to laugh—and sometimes cry when necessary— while we sat around your kitchen table working on this book.

I also want to thank my wife, Charlene, for allowing me to take time away from the family to practice my gift of preaching, teaching and writing. I struggle to put into words how much I appreciate you. If my ministry has in any way touched people's lives with God's love, it has been because of your partnership with me every step of the way.

I also must thank my parents and siblings, many of whom have gone on to glory. Thank you for the formative role you played in shaping my character by putting up with my mistakes and helping me to celebrate my victories.

To the man who spoke about the character of Moses at a business-men's luncheon so many years ago, I owe a debt of gratitude. I never knew you, but your brief message has had a profound and lasting impact on my life.

To my staff and all the great people who call BOSS their church home, this book wouldn't have happened without your encouragement to write. I wrote this book with you in mind. I hope God will use it to speak into your life and continue to build you up as mighty men and women of God.

Special thanks to Karen Davis for doing the final proofreading of the text. It was a labor of love that has made this book better.

Finally, thanks to God for tolerating my foolishness, and allowing me to share with people the experiences and tests you have used to build my character. I know that many times I've learned the hard way. I continue to be a work in progress. But thanks to your incredible mercy and grace, you have always given me another chance.

- Sherwood Carthen

I want to thank Sherwood for his friendship and for the opportunity he has given me to write this book with him. It's been an honor and privilege to be a part of a project I believe will be life-changing for those who take this book to heart.

I also want to thank my wife, Linda. You have been my partner on this project, reading and editing everything I've written. Whether I'm working with you or just standing next to you, you always make me look better.

Finally, to my Mom and Dad, you modeled godly character for me every day and worked lovingly, tirelessly, and too often thanklessly to develop my character. Who I am today largely stands on who you are and always have been. Thanks.

- Phil Sommerville

Foreword

By Kevin Johnson, Mayor of the City of Sacramento, CA

I first met Sherwood Carthen at a chapel service before a Sacramento Kings game at ARCO Arena. I was playing for the Phoenix Suns and, as I usually did before games, I sought out words of wisdom and inspiration from Christ. As the Kings' team chaplain, Bishop Carthen led these chapels and, as I was soon to find out, profoundly impacted those in his sphere of influence. I remember vividly that first chapel service conducted by Bishop Carthen—his eloquent, yet commanding speech, his soft, yet clear demeanor, and most importantly, his challenge to all of us to lead a life of character and become difference-makers in the world.

When Bishop Carthen asked me to write the foreword for his book, *Soul'd Out*, I jumped at the opportunity because there are few men who can convey the importance of living a life of character as well as Bishop Carthen. In *Soul'd Out*, Bishop Carthen leads us down a path of life-changing decisions that establish personal character. At the end of the path, the most important character decision is to be "soul'd out to following Christ." It is Christ who will transform us and build our character.

As Mayor of the City of Sacramento, I certainly relate to Bishop Carthen's call to making life-changing decisions. On a daily basis I am faced with making crucial decisions on behalf of the residents of Sacramento. Before making any decision I carefully weigh the pros and cons, knowing full well that almost certainly some will find fault in whatever I decide. In fact, the pressure to determine what benefits city residents the most has taken on new dimensions in light of the economy's struggles, and requires that I rely upon the strength of my integrity and character. I know I must remain courageous and follow my convictions. Believing in Christ helps me rest assured that I've made the right decision.

Deciding to serve others has long been a staple of Bishop Carthen's approach to strengthening character, and he most certainly practices what he preaches. Throughout the years, I have witnessed Bishop Carthen regularly practice the principles espoused in *Soul'd Out*, and I have watched him unite people for the greater good. Recently, as part of an area-wide initiative called "One-Day to End Homelessness," Bishop Carthen galvanized the faith-based community to help raise private, local funding that ultimately enabled the City of Sacramento to leverage more than $1.5 million in federal support to provide relief for those in need.

Bishop Carthen has helped strengthen my character and provided additional clarity on the importance of making a positive difference in life. Like his efforts to provide an answer to Sacramento's homeless issue, Bishop Carthen fully understands that the role of the faith-based community should not simply be relegated to Sunday services, but extend beyond the walls of the church. Convincing the faith-based community to get involved in critical issues, even when they have political ramifications, is a game-changing decision for the church—one that will benefit congregations and communities citywide. It requires strong character to take such a stand. It is not the easiest approach, but it can be the most impactful.

Soul'd Out should be read by anyone seeking to live a life of significance that is marked by integrity and character. If you desire self-improvement and are willing to take a courageous step, then I encourage you to add *Soul'd Out* to your personal growth toolbox.

Table of Contents

Choices that Define You

"Choices are the hinges of destiny." - Pythagoras

It was a New Year's Eve worship service I'll never forget. Kneeling at the front of the church, a young man was on his knees sobbing. The congregation was taken aback, and I was stunned. You see, this young man was not a church member—he was a hardened gangster, well known to the police, and someone who'd rather be looking for trouble than looking for God.

It was amazing he was even at church that night. He was there only because his mama had "requested" he come with the family on New Year's Eve. As hard as this young man was, he couldn't say no to his mama. As it turns out, he couldn't say no to God either.

When the pastor invited the congregation to make a "soul'd out" commitment to Christ, this young man came stumbling forward, fell to his knees, and said, "Jesus, I need you."

It's always powerful when someone recognizes their need for God and responds to Him, but this was extra special. A gang member wants to be feared. He prides himself on having a reputation for being hard, strong, and intimidating. A gang-banger wouldn't be caught dead looking like he was weak or needy. Yet there was this young man on his knees in front of the church, not caring who saw him, choosing to surrender his life to Christ. But was he serious?

If he was serious, it would mean he was choosing to sell-out his gang in order to be soul'd out to Christ. If he was serious, this moment would not only be the start of a new year, but of a new life. Was he serious, or was this just an emotional moment that would be forgotten by morning? I couldn't be sure.

I'm saddened to tell you this, but only a few weeks later this young man was gunned down in front of his home by a rival gang.

Choices Lead to Consequences

On the day of the funeral, I spoke with the police sergeant in charge of the Sacramento Gang Unit. He shared that parents frequently tell him that their sons have left the gangs, but it's seldom true. These parents are "faking the funk," deceiving themselves, unwilling to face the truth about their children. "So whenever I hear about someone getting out of a gang," he said, "I'm highly skeptical." Then he went on to say, "But this kid was different."

The sergeant told me that this kid was the real deal. He had removed his gang signs, stopped wearing gang colors, and was back in school. "Plus," the sergeant continued, "Whenever we did a 'sting', this kid was nowhere to be found. I have no doubt in my mind that this kid had gotten out of the gang and was turning his life around."

The Bible tells us in 2 Corinthians 5:17 that when we surrender to Jesus, the "old life is gone; a new life has begun!" It was obvious to me that this young man had soul'd out to Christ on New Year's Eve. As a result, he experienced Jesus' power to turn his life around. A "new life had begun." But sadly, his past choices caught up to him.

The police officer told me that on the night this young man was killed, he wasn't even doing anything wrong. He wasn't in the wrong place or with the wrong people. He was shot by rival gang members in retaliation for something his former gang had done long before. The rival gang hadn't heard that their target was now out of the gang. Or maybe they did hear, but they didn't believe it was possible to truly get out, to truly change.

> "Wow," I thought, "you can choose your actions, but you can't choose your consequences."

"Wow," I thought, "you can choose your actions, but you can't choose your consequences."

I don't know what led that young man to make the fatal choice of joining a gang. But it made me wonder—what if he'd made a different choice?

The Choices that Define You

Your choices will make or break you. During your lifetime, you will make some key decisions that will shape your life for better or worse. For example:

- Which school should I attend?
- Who will I marry?
- What career will I pursue?
- Where should I live?

Many people think these decisions are among the most important decisions they'll make in life. People spend countless hours fretting over decisions like these, and spend hard earned dollars on books, magazines and seminars to get advice on how to make these decisions. I promise you, this isn't another book on how to choose the "right one", or how to pick a career that will make you rich or famous. This book goes deeper.

Although decisions about marriage, career, and education are life-altering, they are not the most important decisions you'll ever make. Not even close. No, the most important decisions you'll ever make will be decisions about your character.

It is your character—the total sum of who you are—that guides you as you make decisions in all the important areas of your life. The quality of your life will be determined by the quality of your decisions, but the quality of your decisions will be determined by the quality of your character. That is why character decisions are the most important decisions you will ever make. As Proverbs 11:5 says, "Moral character makes for smooth traveling" (MSG). Amen all by myself.

Being a Difference-Maker

Let me share with you why it is so important to make the right decisions about your character. I have the privilege of being the NBA chaplain for the Sacramento Kings. In the NBA, there are a lot of men with good character, but there are always a few knuckleheads. These knuckleheads are men with enormous talent, but because they have poor character they end up making bad choices both on and off the court.

These bad choices undercut their potential, shorten their careers, damage their relationships, and cost them millions of dollars. But in my mind, that isn't even the greatest loss.

When you blow an opportunity to make the world a better place, you make it a poorer place. That's a failed life.

The greatest loss is their failure to become difference-makers in the world. Professional athletes have tremendous opportunities to make a difference. Because they're admired by others, they can inspire people to be compassionate, generous, courageous, and do great things for a world that has great needs. But because of poor character, some of these athletes rob themselves of this opportunity. That's a tragedy. In fact, it ticks me off. When you blow an opportunity to make the world a better place, you end up making it a poorer place. To me, that's a failure—that's a failed life.

Because your character matters, the decisions you make about your character are of supreme importance. You cannot afford to get these decisions wrong because they will determine whether you will be a person whose life counts for something, or a failure.

The Power of Influence

More likely than not, you're not an NBA player—but you do have influence. You influence people who are watching you when you don't even know they're watching. For example:

You influence friends. Have you ever encouraged a friend to watch a movie or TV show, and they ended up becoming a huge fan? Have you ever inspired someone else to lose weight, start exercising, take a class, or even go to church because they saw you do it with great success? That's influence.

You influence co-workers. When I was a manger with the DMV, I always had new employees work next to the best employees on my team so they would learn how to do the job with excellence. That's influence.

You even influence strangers. Have you ever had someone brighten up your day simply by giving you a smile? Have you ever had a stranger cut you off in traffic and cause your blood pressure to rise? Good or bad, that's influence.

Your greatest influence is with your family. For better or worse, your family has influenced you, and you influence your family. Are you an encouragement or a discouragement? Do you build up or tear down? Do you create an atmosphere of love and support, or fear and insecurity? Either way, you are an influence.

No matter who you are, you have influence for good or bad. The kind of influence you have will be determined by the choices you make, and the choices you make will be determined by your character.

The Sweet & Sour Chicken that Changed my Life

What kind of person will I be? That's the question I was suddenly and unexpectedly confronted with a number of years ago in the back room of a Chinese Buffet. I was there to attend a Christian Businessmen's luncheon. At the time, I was an up-and-coming professional. I had recently been promoted to manager of my department, and was also pastoring a church in my "spare time." My primary purpose for being at this luncheon was to rub shoulders with other ambitious Christian professionals like myself. I had no idea God was about to rock my world.

After we had filled ourselves with sweet and sour chicken, pepper beef and fried rice, the speaker was introduced. As he stood up, I made note of his impeccable dress and confident demeanor. I immediately equated this man with success; and if he was a success, then he probably had something to say that was worth listening to. I sat on the edge of my seat waiting to soak in his nuggets of business wisdom.

I'll never forget what he said. His words have influenced the rest of my life. I expected him to speak on the business practices that made him a success, but instead he spoke on being a man of outstanding character, and he used an obscure Bible passage I had never noticed before.

He spoke from Hebrews 11:24-25 where it says, "It was by faith that Moses, when he grew up, refused to be called the son of Pharaoh's daughter. He chose to share the oppression of God's people instead of enjoying the fleeting pleasures of sin."

Doing the Right Thing

Moses faced a hard choice. He lived in palatial splendor. He wore the best clothes and ate the best food. He had servants to meet his every whim. It was impossible for life to be much more luxurious than his life. I know a lot of people who would be willing to sell-out their lives to gain the kind of wealth and power Moses enjoyed. But if Moses wanted to continue to live a life of royal luxury, it would mean he would be selling-out his Jewish heritage and rejecting God.

On the other hand, if Moses chose to affirm his Jewish heritage, he would be giving up his royal Egyptian upbringing with all its wealth and pleasures. Moses was faced with the choice of living at the top of the pile, or the bottom of the barrel.

Some choice, huh?

When we look at the decision Moses faced, we can see that there was a clear right or wrong decision to be made. But from Moses' perspective, looking out his palace window, wearing his fine, perfectly tailored clothes, with servants standing in the shadows, the choice would probably not have seemed so clear-cut.

Moses couldn't see what the future held. All he saw was a choice between being a royal prince or a Jewish slave—like the ones he could see from his window, toiling in the dust, wearing rags and being ordered around by men with whips.

Moses' career, future, lifestyle, security, circle of friends and much more would all be determined by his decision. Can you imagine a decision more momentous than this one?

For most people, the choice wouldn't be difficult to make. "Palace or slave? Hold the phone and let me think about that one." Most people would sell-out for the money, pleasure and power. We see people making that kind of choice all the time.

If Moses had chosen the fleeting pleasures of sin, he would have squandered his opportunity to be significant."

But if Moses had chosen the life of royalty, we would never have heard from him again. He would have become a forgotten minor prince of Egypt—a nobody. He would also have become a failure who, for the fleeting pleasures of sin, squandered his opportunity to be significant.

To Moses, however, the opposite would have seemed more likely. He was an important prince. If he chose to leave the palace, he would become a nobody. In fact, for a long period of time that's exactly what happened to Moses. He became another unknown nomad out in the desert. But it's funny how God flips the script when you make the right choice.

Moses made the choice "to share the oppression of God's people instead of enjoying the fleeting pleasures of sin." Moses decided: "I'm not going to pursue comfort and pleasure. I'm not going to grab for power and fame. I'm not going to pay attention to those who say I'm crazy. I am a Hebrew! I will choose to do the right thing. I will suffer with my people, rather than enjoy the spoils of kings—spoils that, as a Jew, I am not rightfully entitled to."

Moses made a soul'd-out commitment to his Hebrew roots and embraced the God of his fathers. It was a momentous, life-changing choice that came at an enormous price.

But it was the right choice.

That choice forever shaped Moses' character. He became a man God could use to lead an entire nation out of slavery, a man God could trust to make wise decisions, a man God could empower to bring change to an entire culture and shape the course of history.

I Almost Quit

As I sat in the Chinese Buffet listening to that businessman unpack this obscure verse about Moses, I felt like he was preaching directly to me. Like most young professionals, I was focused on climbing the ladder in pursuit of greater comfort, wealth, and security. Living in the USA, these are the things we are taught to value, and we pursue them with vigor, even at the expense of doing the right thing. But Moses, who had all the wealth and comfort we could ever dream of, chose to give it up instead.

Using these verses from Hebrews, this businessman drove home the necessity of developing godly character. He explained that the decision Moses made wasn't the kind of decision you make on a whim. Moses didn't go to bed a blunder and wake up a wonder. He didn't say out of the blue, "I'm going to leave the palace behind today and choose to be oppressed." The passage specifically states that Moses made this decision "when he grew up." It's as if to say that it took time to develop the character needed to make that momentous, life-altering choice.

As I listened to this man speak, God was speaking—no, thundering—in my soul. I actually began to tremble. It may not have been visible to those around me, but inside I was trembling, because as a pastor I knew I hadn't developed the kind of character this businessman was talking about. What's worse, I didn't even know how.

God was shaking me to the core of my being. Up until then, I thought I'd been doing so well. I thought I was really something. I was one of the youngest men to ever be promoted to manager in my department, and I was serving God as a pastor. I was feeling pretty good about myself.

But now I felt miserable. I had aspirations of climbing the ladder of success, but I suddenly realized that I didn't have what it took to be a success without losing my soul. I didn't have the necessary character.

I began to sulk. Even though I was a preacher, a "mere" businessman was taking me to school. He knew more about godly character—and had more of it—than I did.

I began to question my calling to be a pastor. Who was I to be preaching? Surely I didn't have what it takes. "God," I thought, "you've got the wrong dude." I almost quit. I almost walked away from my calling. But God stopped me in my tracks and showed me that He had brought this businessman and his message across my path not to destroy me, but to show me that I had a choice to make.

Okay, But How?

God was challenging me to improve my character, but now I had a problem. You see, all my life I had been told to have godly character, but no one ever told me how. It seemed like good character was something you either had or you didn't—like pregnancy. I had no idea how to develop godly character. Could it even be developed as an adult? I didn't know.

All my life I had been told to have godly character, but no one told me how.

Now, years later, I look around and see that there are many others who don't know how to build godly character either. As a result, they make poor choices. I've seen the pain and hurt those choices have caused in my congregation, in the NBA, in my community, and in my own family.

When I took up the challenge of developing my character, I didn't know where to start. But gradually I began to learn how to build my character with the help of the Holy Spirit. The lessons I've learned came slowly. Often, I had to come up the rough side of the mountain.

If it weren't for God's grace, and the graciousness of His followers, I would have been buried long ago by my poor choices.

As I learned how to develop my own character, I began to wonder how I could help others develop theirs. I asked myself, "What have I learned that could help the NBA players I have the privilege of serving? How could I help my congregation who mean so much to me? And most important of all, what could I do to help my own children? What could I teach them that will help them build outstanding character and become godly men and women who make a significant difference in the world?

What I have learned is this: we build character by making a handful of crucial decisions that will become the core of who we are as men and women. Once we make those decisions, and they become convictions—a settled part of who we are—they will guide us in making wise choices in all the other big decisions of life.

In this book I will share with you seven crucial, life-changing decisions. If you commit yourself to these decisions, you will, with God's kelp, build great character that will lead to great choices that will result in a life of significance. However, if you fail to make these decisions, my years of ministry have shown me that it will inevitably lead to pain and heartbreak.

I don't want to make the claim that these decisions are an all-inclusive list. You may think of other character decisions you will want to add to your own list. But I am convinced that these decisions are among the most important one's you will ever make. Consider them a starting point for forming a rock-solid foundation on which you can build rock-solid character.

Seven Life-changing Character Decisions

1. Decide to be Courageous.

It took courage for Moses to make the choice to leave the palace. Later, it took courage for him to return to Egypt, stand before Pharaoh and dare to say, "Let my people go!" It also took courage to persevere in leading an often ungrateful and obstinate people to the Promised Land. And it will take courage for you to make the decisions that follow. You must determine whether you want to be courageous or fearful. This decision will shape, for better or worse, every big decision of your life.

2. Decide to Avoid Anger.

Anger is the most destructive force on earth. It will tear apart families, churches, teams, corporations, communities and even countries. Moses himself, while making the decision to be soul'd-out to his Jewish heritage, horribly botched the execution of that decision. Moses saw an Egyptian beating a Hebrew, and in the heat and anger of the moment he murdered the Egyptian. That tragic decision caused Moses to flee Egypt. He would spend years roaming the desert, before God determined that Moses was ready to go back and accomplish His plan.

In my experience as a pastor, I have seen too many people held back from greatness because of their anger. To make great decisions, you must be soul'd out to avoiding anger.

3. Decide to Forgive.

When you've been hurt, forgiving is the last thing you want to do. When you are hurt, what you want to do is get even. However, I have never seen anything do more to transform people's lives than when they choose to forgive. When you are soul'd out to forgiveness, it will lead to decisions that bring freedom and joy. But if you decide not to forgive, it will poison your decision-making and lead to bad choices.

Many people who hear me talk about forgiveness are at first highly skeptical. But I'm begging you to keep an open mind. Take a chance, read the chapter and find out why I believe forgiveness is one of the most important decisions you will ever make.

4. Decide to be Content.

We always seem to want more, and if we're not careful our cravings will lead to a downward spiral of broken marriages, destroyed families, ruined friendships, and worse. In contrast, a person who chooses contentment can relax, enjoy life, be a blessing to others and experience that rare quality of inner peace.

5. Decide to be Generous.

My mother always said, "You can give without loving, but you can't love without giving." We have resources of time, talent and treasure that we can give to help make the world a better place, but we will often hold these things back. We live in fear of losing what we have, and that fear leads to bad decisions. The Bible says that it is "More blessed to give than to receive" (Acts 20:35). God knew what He was talking about. Studies have made clear that those who are generous feel happier, more fulfilled, and even live longer lives.

6. Decide to be a Servant.

Proverbs 16:18 says, "Pride goes before destruction," and that saying has proven to be true over and over again. We can all think of examples. However, there is an antidote to pride—serving. Moses had a lot to be proud of, but if he had allowed himself to be prideful he would have made a disastrous choice. Somewhere along the line Moses made the decision to serve others, and that led to making the right choice about leaving the palace and taking his stand with his Jewish brothers. The same will be true for you.

7. Decide to be Soul'd Out to Christ.

I hope that as you read this book you will be convinced of the importance of making these crucial character decisions. But where will you find the fuel you need follow through and stick with these decisions once you make them? God is inviting you to have a strong, personal relationship with Him, that comes complete with the fuel you need to truly commit yourself to these decisions. That's what makes the decision to be soul'd out to following Christ the most important decision you will ever make.

The apostle Paul tells us in Galatians 4:19 that Christ is being "fully developed" in us. When we cooperate with the work God wants to do in us, when we are soul'd out to following Him, He will transform us and build our character.

What will a person who is soul'd out to Christ look like? They will have courageous faith, resist anger, be forgiving, experience contentment, give generously, and serve others. When we are soul'd out to Christ we will be committed to all of these character decisions. We will become people of outstanding character, able to make choices that will make our lives and our world better.

"Shut the Front Door"

It's been my observation that most of us try to sit on the fence when we are faced with difficult decisions. We'd like to have the one thing, but don't want to give up the other. We want it both ways. Hear me clearly on this: when you sit on the fence, you stand for nothing.

Because you are too fearful to do anything, you accomplish nothing. Because no one can count on you, you're not able to make a positive difference. When you sit on the fence you're a sell-out because you're not sold-out to anything.

Sitting on the fence will not make your life better. Instead, it will make you miserable. If you want to be significant, you must choose to be sold-out to something. But this is where the challenge comes, because we can be sold-out to the wrong things.

Your choices will define you. They will make your life better or worse. So, as I say to my church, "Shut the front door." Don't let this opportunity to experience a better life pass you by. The following chapters will help you make character decisions that will lead to better choices. By making better choices, you will experience better consequences. As a result, you will become a person who will be significant, who will make a difference, who will make the world around you better.

Decide to be Courageous

"Life shrinks or expands in proportion to one's courage."
- The Diary of Anais Nin

One small act of courage can change a life, a family, a community, and even history...

It was getting dark on a winter's day, when a neatly dressed woman stepped out of the rain and onto a bus after a day of work. There was nothing unusual about this woman, or about the day, or about her being on the bus. This was her normal routine. She'd been coming to this same bus stop, at this same time, to climb onto this same bus, day after day for years.

As she took her seat, she was thinking about the things that had happened at work and what she needed to do to get dinner fixed when she got home. For her, this was just another bus ride home. She had no idea that in a few minutes she would make a small, but courageous decision that would change history.

With each passing stop, more passengers piled onto the bus until some had to stand in the aisle. On a rainy day this was to be expected. The bus driver, looking back, noticed the standing passengers. So, he pulled himself out of his seat and started to walk down the aisle, pushing his way around disgruntled passengers. Halfway back, the driver grabbed a sign that said, "Colored People Only," and moved it one row further back.

Then, in his thick southern drawl, he told the black passengers sitting in that row that they would have to get up and stand in the back of the bus so that the white people could have their seats. The driver didn't expect any trouble because, sadly, this was the normal way things were done in the South in the 1950's. What wasn't normal was to have a dignified, neatly dressed, and unexpectedly strong-willed black lady simply say, "No, I don't think I should have to stand up."

As Rosa Parks tells the story, the bus driver responded by saying, "Well, if you don't stand up, I'm going to have to call the police and have you arrested." Rosa Parks responded to the dumbfounded driver by simply saying, "You may do that."

The rest, as they say, is history. Rosa Parks' courageous decision was the spark that mobilized the black community of Montgomery, Alabama. Within days they organized the Montgomery Bus Boycott and chose a young, new pastor to the city, the Rev. Martin Luther King Jr., to be the leader. Suddenly, 40,000 passengers—70% of the bus company's customers—stopped riding the bus. The boycott lasted a year, putting drivers out of work and nearly bankrupting the bus company. The city finally relented, changed its laws and desegregated the bus lines. Inspired by this victory, African-Americans around the country began standing up for their rights, and America began to change.

One small act of courage can change a life, a family, a community, and even history.

Success...

You don't have to read between the lines to recognize that courage is a theme that runs throughout the Bible. Joseph had the courage to overcome betrayal, resist temptation, fight off discouragement and rise to an unexpected position of power that allowed him to save God's chosen people from starvation.

Moses needed courage to stand before the most powerful man in the world and demand that he free his slave force. Joshua was "strong and courageous" in leading the conquest of the Promised Land. Gideon courageously obeyed God and defeated an army of tens of thousands with only 300 men armed with horns and torches—not exactly weapons of mass destruction.

David courageously fought the giant Goliath. Esther risked her life to go before the king to stop a massacre the king had ordered. Daniel had the courage to accept the lion's den, and his friends the fiery furnace, rather than worship a human king as if he were God.

Mary, the mother of Jesus, when told she would conceive a child through the Holy Spirit, courageously told the angel of the Lord, "Let it be to me as you have said." Peter dared to walk on water. Paul endured beatings, imprisonment and shipwrecks to tell people about Jesus.

Without a doubt, God uses courageous people to change lives, families, communities and even history. Courage expands your life. It allows you to become a person of significance, a person of substance, a person who makes a difference. If you want to succeed in life, courage will be an absolutely necessary character trait.

...or Failure

However, a lack of courage will lead to failure in life. Vincent Van Gogh once asked, "What would life be if we had no courage to attempt anything?" Again, the Bible gives us many examples of what life is like when we fail to have courage.

What would life be if we had no courage to attempt anything?

Eve didn't have the courage to stand up to the serpent in the Garden of Eden, and her husband, Adam, lacked the courage to stop her from eating the forbidden fruit. From that failure of courage, history was changed, but not for the better.

The nation of Israel, after following Moses out of Egypt, lacked the courage to enter the Promised Land. They were paralyzed with fear after hearing about how powerful the people were who lived there. As a result of their failure, they spent the next forty years wandering in the wilderness until every fearful adult was dead.

Israel's first king, Saul, was commanded to wait before going into battle until the prophet Samuel came to offer a sacrifice to God. However, fearing the desertion of his army, Saul lacked the courage to wait for Samuel. He offered the sacrifice himself. As a result, God rejected Saul as king and chose David to replace him.

Jesus also told a story about a person who lacked courage. In this story, a business owner gave three employees accounts to manage while he was away. Two of the employees made shrewd investments with their master's accounts, and doubled his money. The third employee, however, did nothing with his account. The man was unwilling to take any risks with the owner's money because he was afraid of the owner's reaction if the investments failed. In the end, the owner fired this employee for lacking the courage to use the resources that had been entrusted to him.

There is no doubt that a lack of courage diminishes life. How many great careers have never been launched because people lacked the courage to take a difficult class, make a daring proposal, or risk doing something new? How many dreams have gone unfulfilled and how many people have settled for mediocrity because of their unwillingness to risk failure?

A lack of courage not only diminishes our own lives, it also diminishes life around us. Because of a lack of courage, people will stand by and do nothing when others are abused, and say nothing when others are cheated. Because of a lack of courage people will tolerate destructive behavior and let destructive ideas go unchallenged. It's been said that, "All that is necessary for evil to succeed is for good men to do nothing."

Let me push this even further. Because of a lack of courage, some followers of Christ never tell their friends that Jesus can make a difference in their lives. Maybe they are afraid to tell others because they realize Jesus hasn't changed their own lives. And maybe their own lives haven't changed because they lacked the courage to be soul'd out to Jesus. That's something worth thinking about.

Your life shrinks or expands in proportion to your courage.

Your life shrinks or expands in proportion to your courage. People with courage change lives, families, communities and even history. I am looking for men and women like that. I am looking for men and women who will rise up and be significant!

Do it Scared

Nike's famous slogan is "Just do it." But I want to amend that slogan to say, "Do it scared." Fear, if we let it, can be a destructive force in our life. It can lead us to make bad decisions and keep us from taking the risks necessary to realize our potential. Because we fear failure, we never try to do great things. Because we fear what others think, we never express ourselves. Because we fear rejection, we never reach out.

Courage doesn't take away those fears, but it gives us the strength to overcome them. I define courage as having the willpower to stand up and do what is right, even though you are afraid, and even though it would be much easier to quit.

It takes courage to tell the truth, love someone, be generous, do what's right, or stand against what's wrong. It takes courage to forgive and ask for forgiveness, raise children, quit a destructive habit, or serve others. It takes courage to face tough times. And it takes courage to follow Jesus.

Courage Drives Tenacity

Life is not fair! I hope that isn't news to you, but I keep running into people who act as if they are the only ones who haven't been treated fairly. I want to slap them and say, "Get over it!" But then I remember I'm a pastor.

The reality is that we don't all get the same opportunities. We're not all born in the same place. We don't all receive the same advantages. Bad things happen, even to good people. I'm not saying that's right. I'm saying it's the truth.

People have this assumption that everyone is supposed to get the same opportunities and have the same access to things. They blame their lack of success on not being given the opportunities others have been given, or not having the advantages others enjoy. They excuse their failures because they were "dealt a bad hand." Some people go so far as to say that their bad behavior is justified because of the bad things that have happened to them. These people end up sitting around wasting their lives as they wait for a break, hoping they'll win the lottery.

When bad things happen, you don't give up, you get back up. That's called tenacity. Tenacity keeps you from giving up when the odds are stacked against you, it gets you to stand up after you've been knocked down, and it keeps you moving forward against forces that would hold other people back. Successful people all share this trait of tenacity, and the engine that powers tenacity is courage.

Someone dear to me, I'll call her Vickie, was dealt a bad hand in life. During the crucial formative years of her life, her dad was a knucklehead. I don't know how else to describe him. His daughter loved and adored him, but he spent her growing up years either high on drugs or in jail.

All those years of wanting the love of her daddy, but never experiencing it, left a hole in Vickie's life that could have crushed her. And it almost did. She was spiraling down the "life-is-not-fair" road. She was giving up on life and making bad decisions.

As a pastor, I've seen this story of failure play out again and again in people's lives. But this story is different. Vickie became courageous and pulled out of her tailspin. She went back to school to get her GED, then went on to college and even graduate school. That's what courage looks like. Courage says, "I don't have to accept the hand I was dealt."

It might be hard to change. It might be hard to go back to school. It might be hard to look for a new job. It might be hard to trust again.

It might be hard to love again. Some days, it's hard just getting out of bed. But courage gives you the strength to overcome! It makes you tenacious.

Courage Fuels Integrity

There are going to be times in your life where your integrity is going to be put to a severe test. There are going to be moments where people are going to try to either entice you or pressure you to compromise. In those moments, as you teeter on the brink, you're going to need courage to take a stand.

You've probably watched television shows or movies where a group of conspirators meet in a back room to cut a shady deal that will be good for them personally, but bad for those they represent. I've seen plenty of shows like that and I used to think, "That doesn't really happen." I know differently now. I now know things like that happen, because I was once offered one of those back room deals.

It was the early 1990s and I had just quit my job with the California DMV in order to become a full-time pastor. I believed, and still believe, that part of my job as a pastor is to be active in doing things that will improve the community. In the 1990s, one of the big issues was tobacco use. Tobacco was the number one preventable disease in our community, killing more people than car accidents, AIDS, and drug abuse combined. If we could stop people from smoking, we would save lives. So, I took on the cause of tobacco prevention.

In the 1980s, one out of three people in California were tobacco users. Concerned about the escalating health costs associated with this high rate of tobacco use, the state took a novel approach by heavily taxing tobacco products and giving the money to community organizations, especially minority organizations, to use on tobacco prevention programs. The plan was very successful, cutting tobacco use to less than one out of four people.

By the mid 1990s, the U.S. Department of Health took note of California's success and proposed a national tobacco tax, with the tax money to go to funding anti-tobacco programs across the nation. The tobacco industry, facing the potential loss of billions of dollars, decided to do everything they could to stop this tax, including offering some questionable deals.

The tobacco industry began to meet with African-American, Latino, and Asian community leaders who were involved with tobacco prevention. They believed these leaders would be influential with members of congress. At that time, I was the Chair of the National African-American Tobacco Education Network, and the tobacco industry invited me to Washington D.C.

It was an all-expense paid trip. When we arrived, we were wined and dined, and then we met in a—you guessed it—back room. I sat at a table with a small group of black leaders from around the country and listened to representatives of the tobacco industry make an offer they hoped we couldn't refuse.

They said, "If you will lobby against this proposed tobacco tax, we will pour money into your communities that you can use in any way you want. On top of that, we will also make sure that money will go into your own pockets as well." I'm not talking about Kibbles & Bits money. I'm talking about millions of dollars that they were willing to divide among those of us sitting in that back room.

I'd like to tell you that my very first reaction was, "Oh no! God Forbid! The Devil is Alive! I can't do that!" But it wasn't like that. I had to swallow hard a few times as I thought

> *"If you will lobby against the tobacco tax, we will pour money into your pockets." I'm talking millions.*

about the amount of money being offered. I was tempted, really tempted to shake hands and take the money. I took a big salary drop when I quit the DMV to become a full-time pastor, and I really needed that money.

But I couldn't do it. I would not have been able to live with myself. I would have been a sell-out. I would have corrupted my integrity and sold-out my community for a fistful of dollars. When you say yes to something like that, you have to start covering up what you've done. You have to start hiding things. Once you do that, your character gets chipped away until it finally collapses and takes your life down with it.

Without courage, I could not have said no to that offer. I was not only dazzled by the amount of money they wanted to slip into my pockets, I was also feeling the heat from others in the room who wanted to take the deal. You see, this was an all-or-nothing offer. We all had to agree to the deal. They couldn't afford the risk of someone spilling the beans and pointing fingers.

I'm not happy to say this, but there were some people in our group who wanted the money. They were not at all happy with those of us who were saying no. These were national leaders. I was feeling the heat, but stood firm.

To the disappointment of our hosts, the meeting ended without our agreement to their offer. As we got up to leave, the lady sitting next to me, thinking of the money we had just turned down, turned and asked me, "Pastor, what did we just do?"

I said, "I think we did what was right."

I wonder sometimes what my life would be like now if I had accepted that boatload of money. Would I be living on easy street, financially secure, enjoying the nice things of life? But then I think, "I'm not even sure if that deal was legit. I could be in jail right now." Then, I remind myself of all the things God has allowed me to do since that time. If I had compromised my integrity back then, I am certain God would never have given me these opportunities.

There's a lot at stake when our integrity is on the line, usually more than we can imagine. But if we make the decision to always be courageous, we will have the fuel needed to maintain our integrity under pressure.

Courage Leads to Significance.

I may never have met you, but I know we have something in common. We both want to be significant in some way. I know this, because the need to be significant is universal. No one wants to feel worthless. When people feel like their lives are meaningless they lose hope, fall into a deep depression and give up on life. We all have a desire to be significant. Don't you agree?

I believe this universal desire for significance points to the existence of God, because God created us to be significant. Ephesians 2:10 says, "For we are God's handiwork, created in Christ Jesus to do good works, which God prepared in advance for us to do" (NIV).

The word translated as "handiwork" in this verse has the meaning of exquisite workmanship, something made by a master craftsman. You see, we are significant because we are exquisitely made by God. Going further, we are also significant because we have a God-given purpose and calling. God created us to do a significant work that He "prepared in advance" for us to do.

But there's a catch. Our significance is based entirely on our connection to God. We are significant because we are created and treasured by God. However, when our relationship with God is damaged, it damages our sense of significance.

As a result, we start to look for something else that will make us feel significant. To find significance, we look to money, or relationships, or power, or sex, or work. But all these things come up short because they all can be lost or taken away. These things don't provide a solid foundation for significance.

We will only truly experience our significance when we are soul'd out to God and decide to step up and do God's work. However, stepping up to God's call is going to take courage

Soul'd Out Courage

You will not find a person in the Bible who didn't need courage to answer God's call. Many of them were afraid to do what God was

> *You will not find a person in the Bible who didn't need courage to answer God's call.*

calling them to do. Saul tried to hide himself in a pile of luggage rather than be named king (1 Samuel 10:22). The prophet Isaiah, one of the greatest prophets of the Bible, responded to

God's call by saying, "Woe is me" (Isaiah 6:5). Moses said, "Here I am, God—send someone else!" (Exodus 4:13).

Noah needed courage to build the Ark. Nehemiah needed courage to rebuild the walls of Jerusalem. The apostle Paul needed courage to go on his missionary journeys. The early Christians needed courage to endure persecution. You will need courage to be soul'd out to following Jesus. And until you are soul'd out, you will never discover your true significance.

When you are soul'd out to Jesus, people will notice and react. Some will think you're foolish, others will think you're weak. Some will laugh at you, others will insult you. Some will avoid you, others will disown you. It will take courage to keep from caving-in under all the negative reactions you'll receive from friends and strangers.

When you are soul'd out to Jesus, you will change as you break bad habits and create new ones. Your language may change. Your activities may change. Your choice of entertainment may change. As you change, you will be leaving comfort zones, and that, too, takes courage.

It takes courage to step up and do the "good works which God prepared in advance for us to do." You will have to break out of your lethargy and get up from your La-Z-Boy. You will need to give up things in your life and rearrange your schedule. You will have to rub shoulders with strangers. You will need to do things that won't come with a guarantee of success. But as you start taking advantage of opportunities to serve, you will discover your significance.

Courage is Built on En-*courage*-ment

Joey grew up on a steady diet of criticism. "How could you be so stupid?" "What is wrong with you?" "You're a clumsy oaf!" "You're totally worthless" "Are you going to school looking that ugly?" "You must have a different daddy, cuz I know I couldn't have a son as dumb as you are."

Not surprisingly, Joey grew up believing he was worthless. He was unwilling to try things because he was preprogrammed to believe he would fail. He never married because he was too insecure. He was never a success. He never had the courage to pursue his dreams. He didn't even have enough courage to have a dream. Joey never had courage, because Joey never experienced love.

Love builds a foundation of courage. When you grow up being loved, you believe you are lovable, and that belief gives you courage. You are able to take the risk of loving others because you know that even if they reject you, you'll be okay, because you know that you are lovable.

Andrea's parents told her how proud they were of her and how much they loved her. They encouraged her efforts even when the results were marginal. When she failed, they told her they believed she would accomplish great things. When she was heartbroken, they told her about all the incredible things they admired in her.

Although Andrea wasn't the prettiest, smartest or wealthiest girl in school, she was well-liked, had many friends, laughed easily, and was willing to try new things. Unlike Joey, Andrea went on to have a successful career and a happy marriage.

What made the difference in Andrea's life? En-*courage*-ment. When you receive a steady diet of encouragement like Andrea received, it builds a foundation of courage.

If you are a parent, you can raise courageous kids by filling them with love and encouragement. So, pay attention to your words. Pay attention to your physical responses. Give hugs instead of eye rolls, positive reinforcement instead of condemnation.

You can also build courage in your friends by encouraging them. Let your friends know what you admire about them. Tell them about the strengths you see in them. When they take a risk to stretch them-selves, cheer them on. When they fail, let them know they still have a friend who believes in them.

Likewise, when you have encouraging friends, you'll develop the courage to be successful. If you don't have friends like that, you need to get them. But rather than waiting for them to come to you, show a little courage and be a friend like that to others. You might just change a life.

The Ultimate Source of Courage

But what if you are more of a Joey than an Andrea? You've grown up in a harsh environment with little love. You have few friends and the ones you have are negative. Where will you find your courage?

Our ultimate source of courage is found in God. Don't ever forget that you are "God's handiwork." Just as a painting has great worth because it was painted by a master, you have great worth because you were exquisitely created by *the* Master. So no matter what you have heard from your family, school, friends or workplace, know that you are a masterpiece.

You may have trouble recognizing that you're a masterpiece be-cause you've been tarnished, dirtied, and beat up by the sins you've committed, or by the sins others have committed against you. But God sees the treasure under the tarnish. He knows who He made you to be, and treasures you so much that He came to earth to personally claim you with His own blood. You can find your foundation of courage in

God's love, if you will accept His love and commit yourself to following Him.

Faith in God and courage are intricately tied together. In fact, courage is nothing more than faith in action. Let me share a biblical example.

The Israelites were at war with the Philistines, and things were looking grim. Every day, the Philistines would form their battle lines and viciously taunt and ridicule the Israelite army. In response, the Israelites did... nothing. In fact they cowered in fear. It was embarrassing.

The Philistines had a reason for being courageous. They had the biggest, baddest warrior on the block, a behemoth named Goliath. It is easy to be brave when you're standing next to the biggest, baddest guy around.

Then, David showed up.

David was unafraid of Goliath because he believed that *he* was standing next to the biggest, baddest guy in the universe—God. When David stepped out from Israel's battle lines, Goliath rubbed his eyes in disbelief, amazed that someone so young and so, well, puny was going to attempt to fight him.

Goliath started to laugh, and his laughter rumbled like thunder through the valley. Undeterred, David began to run at Goliath, swinging his slingshot over his head. Goliath was probably still laughing as David let the fateful stone fly. Then the laughing stopped. In just seconds, Israel's army suddenly became en-couraged, and the Philistines ran in terror. The rout was on.

Faith in God gave David courage. Later in his life, David wrote, "Even though I walk through the darkest valley, I will fear no evil, for you are with me" (Psalm 23:4).

Joshua 1:9 says, "Be strong and courageous. Do not be afraid; do not be discouraged, for the LORD your God will be with you

We have God on our side! When you believe that...you'll have an unshakeable foundation of courage.

wherever you go." Romans 8:31 asks, "If God is for us, who can be against us?" 1 John 4:4 says, "You have overcome them, because the one who is in you is greater than the one who is in the world" (NIV).

We have God on our side! When you believe that, with inner conviction, you will have an unshakeable foundation of courage.

Strengthening Your Courage

Too often we equate courage with some giant act of bravery—the fireman who runs into a burning building to save a child, the soldier going into battle, the pastor getting up to preach. Well, maybe not that last one, although surveys do say that most people are more afraid of public speaking than they are of dying.

The courage of heroes, however, didn't come to them suddenly. Their courage was built one step at a time through training, repetition and trusting the people around them. Our courage is built up the same way—one step at a time. Pastor and author, Chuck Swindoll, said,

"Courage is not limited to the battlefield or the Indianapolis 500, or bravely catching a thief in your house. The real tests of courage are much deeper and much quieter. They are the inner tests, like remaining faithful when nobody's looking, like enduring pain when the room is empty, like standing alone when you're misunderstood."

It is through small, daily acts of courage that we build our courage "muscle." With every act of courage, we become more courageous. When the moment that tests our integrity and tenacity comes, we'll find we have the courage we need because of the accumulation of all the small acts of courage we've shown in the past.

So what are these small acts of courage that can strengthen us? For some of us, just choosing to get up in the morning will be a good start. But beyond that, here are a few suggestions:

- Look for the positive in any situation.
- Be encouraging in a discouraging environment.
- Don't tell a lie when it would be advantageous to do so.
- Care for someone even when you don't have the time or inclination.
- Do something healthy, and stop doing something unhealthy.
- Offer to pray for someone.
- Bite your tongue when you're about to say something unkind.
- Do the right thing when no one is watching.
- Stand up for someone being picked on or joked about.
- Be friendly to the shy person who needs a friend, but doesn't have the courage to make one.

These suggestions will get you warmed up. Now build on them. With every act of courage, you will become more courageous.

You Must Choose

There will be times in your life when you will be tested. You will be tempted by pleasure, wealth, fame, comfort, or even fear. Will you have the courage to do the right thing, or will you be a sell-out? If you lack the courage to do the right thing it will have damaging repercussions that will last for years, even generations. But if you have the courage to do the right thing, no matter how difficult it will be, you can change a life, a family, a community, and even history. It's your choice.

Decide to Resist Anger

"Anger, if not restrained, is frequently more hurtful to us than the injury that provoked it." - Seneca

I was an angry young man. There, I said it, and it's true.

My anger stemmed from when I had been molested as a child. I was young, small and powerless, and an evil person had taken advantage of me. But when I became a teenager, I was no longer powerless. I was physically strong, and I vowed that I would never again allow anyone to take advantage of me. I also took it as my duty to never allow a bully to take advantage of my friends or siblings.

I began to learn that I could use my size and the sheer volume of my voice to intimidate others. I also learned how to fight. I became the bully to the bullies, and I unleashed my anger on anyone who dared to try taking advantage of me or my friends.

I don't want to give you the wrong impression. I wasn't a walking cauldron of hot, molten anger ready to explode at a moment's notice. Most of the time, I was a nice guy. But the anger was there under the surface, and it broke through far too frequently.

I hated the feeling of powerlessness. But whenever I felt like I wasn't getting my own way, I would feel powerless, and that triggered my anger. To gain back power, I used intimidation. First, I used my size to tower over people and glower at them. If that wasn't enough, I started yelling. I found that most people didn't want to mess with a very large, loud, and angry man. So, I usually got my way.

I realized, however, that my anger did not give me what I wanted most—love and respect. People feared me, but they didn't respect me. When I walked into a room, people would run for cover. I created havoc at work and at home. I wasn't making things better, I was making them worse. The anger I thought was protecting me was actually destroying everything I valued.

The Angry Decision

Anger leads to terrible decision-making. When you're angry, you short-circuit clear thinking. You begin to interpret everything through a distorted lens. You perceive slights that don't exist. You become overly suspicious. You're pessimistic instead of optimistic. You overreact to innocent comments and actions.

Anger makes a mess out of your life. I have witnessed too many people held back from achieving greatness because of their anger. Too many people have destroyed marriages, families, friendships and careers because of anger. I was one of those people. Because of my anger, I put my marriage and my job in jeopardy.

I have learned the hard way that one of the most important decisions you will ever make is the decision to avoid anger. And when anger can't be avoided, you must learn how to let go of it in healthy ways. When you make the decision to live without anger and act on that decision every day, it will transform your life.

The Danger of Anger

Jesus wanted to make sure we clearly understood the corrosive danger of anger. In the Sermon on the Mount, He taught:

You have heard that our ancestors were told, "You must not murder. If you commit murder, you are subject to judgment." But I say, if you are even angry with someone, you are subject to judgment! If you call someone an idiot, you are in danger of being brought before the court. And if you curse someone, you are in danger of the fires of hell.

So if you are presenting a sacrifice at the altar in the Temple and you suddenly remember that someone has something against you, leave your sacrifice there at the altar. Go and be reconciled to that person. Then come and offer your sacrifice to God.

When you are on the way to court with your adversary, settle your differences quickly. Otherwise, your accuser may hand you over to the judge, who will hand you over to an officer, and you will be thrown into prison. (Matthew 5:21-25)

Jesus started this passage by quoting one of the Ten Commandments: "You must not murder." But then Jesus took things a step further to essentially say: "You know the commandment, but let me show you the spirit behind the commandment." Anger is what is behind murder. So, even though you may be murder-free, if you are living in anger you're still sinning. Anger is a warning signal that your heart is not right with God." Ouch!

Jesus is very clear: a person soul'd out to Him will refuse to live with anger. If you want to become the person God created you to be, you have to learn how to deal with your anger.

> *Jesus is very clear: a person soul'd out to Him will refuse to live with anger.*

Learning to Avoid Anger

First, let me say that not all anger can be avoided. When people do harmful things to you, anger is natural. My own anger was the result of a heinous evil done to me—it was justified. In fact, I believe God was angry about what happened to me because God is angered by evil. In some instances anger can even be healthy. Great things have been achieved in the world because anger moved people to take action against an injustice.

However, when mismanaged, anger can cause great damage. If we choose to cling to it, we will sell-out to the anger and destroy everything that is most valuable to us.

Sometimes we try to deal with our anger by denying it. We try to stuff it down and hide it from of our consciousness in an effort to keep it from harming us. We try to convince ourselves that we are not angry. This does more harm than good. Denying anger not only causes depression and physical ailments, it allows anger to build until it erupts in the most destructive ways possible. You will be far better off to admit your anger and deal with it than to deny your anger.

If you are a person who constantly struggles with anger, I suggest that you skip ahead to the next chapter in order to learn how to let God deal with it. Then, when you finish that chapter, you can return to this chapter to learn how to avoid it.

Aim for Peace

I have found that the best place to start when it comes to avoiding anger is to aim for something else. A mountain biking friend taught me this lesson. He explained that subconsciously we always head in the direction we're looking. In other words, if you're mountain biking, and you're focused on the rocks in your path, odds are you're going to hit those rocks. Instead of focusing on the rocks, you want to focus on the path around the rocks.

This lesson applies to anger as well. Instead of focusing on the anger you want to avoid, focus on something else. But what should we focus on? The Bible gives us a good idea. 1 Peter 3:10-11 says, "If you want to enjoy life and see many happy days...search for peace and work to maintain it." The meaning is clear: if you want to avoid anger, focus on making peace. Jesus taught us the same lesson in the Sermon on the Mount when he said, "God blesses those who work for peace" (Matthew 5:9). The question now becomes: how do we make peace?

Tell the Truth...In Love

First, a peacemaker tells the truth. They call a spade a spade. But they do it with love. A peacemaker doesn't use the truth like a sledgehammer. They don't try to use the truth to shame or harm an enemy. Instead, a peacemaker will speak the truth in a way that opens doors to reconciliation and healing.

This means that peacemakers are careful about the words they use and the actions they take. Their goal is to make peace rather than exact revenge. So, they try to avoid hurtful words and actions.

Proverbs 13:3 says, "Those who control their tongue will have a long life; opening your mouth can ruin everything." I once was the poster boy for this verse. I'd open my mouth and before you knew it the room was in an uproar.

When I was in my 20s, I worked as a Supervisor with the California Department of Motor Vehicles. One of my employees was a single mom who could barely pay her bills. In order to help her, I arranged for overtime opportunities in our office to go to her first. This arrangement seemed to work well, and it helped someone with real needs.

All that changed, however, when my boss sent out a memo. It said all overtime opportunities would need to be shared equally with everyone in the office.

My boss's decision was going to cause a lot of harm to the single mom in my office. Without the extra overtime, she might not be able to stay in her apartment or feed her kids. How dare my boss create a hardship for this employee! Because I saw myself as a protector of the powerless, my anger button had been pushed.

What doubled my anger was that my boss didn't consult me before making her decision. It didn't matter that she, as my boss, had every right to make this decision on her own. She still should have consulted ME! I was not getting my way and that added to my anger.

Remember how I said anger leads to poor decision-making? Well, my next action certainly proved that to be true. After reading the memo, I was so angry I immediately jumped up from my desk and headed for my supervisor's office. Too angry to even wait for the elevator, I pounded up the stairs. With each step, I rehearsed the choice words I was going to say. I was a mama bear whose cub was in danger.

I barged into my boss's office unannounced, pounded my fists down on her desk, leaned forward, gave her my best glare, and then unleashed my verbal onslaught. I was going to make sure I got my way. When I finished, I continued to glare down on my boss, waiting for her to cave in to my expectations.

Instead, she sharply said, "Sit down!" It came across like a slap in the face. I was stunned.

Once seated, she told me, "I don't know how many other people you can intimidate like that, but you're not going to intimidate me. Busting in here like that with your loud voice and your angry demeanor isn't going to change the situation. And if you don't do something about your anger, you're not going to be working here much longer."

My angry words nearly cost me my job. Thank God I had a boss who was a peacemaker. She firmly told me the truth in a way that wasn't angry, but certainly got my attention. Because she told the truth in love, I realized that I needed to deal with my anger.

Language Counts

When our goal is to make peace, we will respond differently to people who have slighted us. Instead of a knee-jerk, tit-for-tat reaction, we will respond in a way that can turn the situation around and create peace. The book of Proverbs is filled with good advice for making peace.

"A gentle answer deflects anger,
but harsh words make tempers flare" (Proverbs 15:1).

"Kind words are like honey—
sweet to the soul and healthy for the body" (Proverbs 16:24).

The words you choose will go a long way towards making peace and avoiding anger. When your focus is peace, your words will be soft, concerned and caring rather than harsh, vengeful or accusatory.

Think of it like this. It's as if each of us is given two buckets to carry around with us—one filled with water and the other filled with gasoline. Each time we encounter a fire, we have the choice of which bucket to pour on the fire. In other words, each time I encounter a situation that makes me angry, I have the choice to pour kind and gentle words, or to pour harsh and angry words. One leads to peace, the other leads to a raging wildfire.

Developing God-Given Anger Repellant

Prayer will also create peace, and not just ordinary peace, it will bring God's peace. Philippians 4:6-7 states, "Do not be anxious about anything, but in every situation, by prayer and petition, with thanksgiving, present your requests to God. And the *peace of God*, which transcends all understanding, *will guard your hearts and your minds* in Christ Jesus (*Emphasis mine*). God's peace is supernatural. It transcends understanding. It helps you avoid anger by guarding your heart and mind. You can think of it as an anger repellant that works inside of you to stop anger before it gets started.

This supernatural peace comes through prayer—a powerful weapon for dealing with anger. When we pray, we make ourselves available to God, and can access His power to avoid anger. When you are in a situation where you feel anger starting to rise, rather than taking a deep breath or counting to ten, say a prayer. When you are around someone who often makes you angry, say a prayer. Let God's power repel the anger.

Here's another tip: when you pray, focus on God more than you focus on the person or situation that angers you. In order to focus on God, start your prayers by praising Him. For example, praise God for His strength, love, forgiveness, or protection. Next, confess your tendency to get angry. Then ask God to fill you with His peace and help you make a wise, peace-making response.

These types of prayers don't have to be long. In fact, when you feel your anger rapidly coming on, a short prayer is probably better. You can pray a prayer like the one above in less time than it will take you to read this paragraph. When you make a habit of praying in situations that trigger your anger, you'll discover those situations

> *Something as simple as thankfulness can be powerfully effective in avoiding anger.*

are bothering you less and less. Increasingly, you'll be able to avoid the anger you previously experienced in those situations.

The Power of being Thankful

Thankfulness is an often missed ingredient for experiencing God's peace. Philippians 4:6-7 clearly states that we need to pray "with thanksgiving." This may surprise you, but something as simple as thankfulness can be powerfully effective in avoiding anger.

Anger is often the result of feeling deprived. Because we don't have the same stuff, opportunities, talent, or looks as someone else, we get angry. You know I'm telling the truth. The problem is with our focus. We're angry because we're focused on what we wish we had rather than on what we already have.

Thankfulness helps us avoid this anger by putting our focus on what we have, not on what we lack. There is no room for anger when we are filled with gratitude. Then, if we express our gratitude in prayer, God will fill us with His peace and give us power to resist anger. So, next time you feel your anger rise, pause and think of something you are thankful for: then say a prayer. You may be surprised at how much this will help you.

When You're Right and They're Wrong

Not only do we need to take steps to avoid anger, we also need to take steps to make peace with those who are angry with us. Look again at what Jesus said in the Sermon on the Mount. "So if you are presenting a sacrifice at the altar in the Temple and you suddenly remember that someone has something against you, leave your sacrifice there at the altar. Go and be reconciled to that person. Then come and offer your sacrifice to God" (Matthew 5:23-24).

Peacemaking means working out your disagreements with others. If you don't work out disagreements they will simmer under the surface until they boil over. That's not the way to avoid anger.

All disagreements have the same simple reason at their root. We disagree because the other person is not bright enough to realize that we're right and they're wrong. There may be a few rare instances where we know we might be wrong, but even then we won't admit it, because that would put us at a disadvantage. You know I'm telling it straight.

Pride, selfishness and fear get in the way of making peace. When my goal is to get my way at the expense of your desires, I've just created anger not peace. When my goal is to be right no matter the cost, I may win the argument but still lose because of the turmoil I've created. I remember when God taught me this lesson.

My wife, Charlene, and I were having a disagreement that could have been quickly resolved. All my wife had to do was agree that I was right. My wife, not surprisingly, didn't see it that way. Rather than being a peacemaker, I was content to let the disagreement simmer until my wife came around to my way of thinking. Although I sensed in my spirit that God was telling me to straighten things out, I was dragging my feet.

It was my wife, not me, who took the initiative to be a peacemaker. One day she said, "Let's go for a walk and talk about this disagreement." So we walked and talked, but I was being uncooperative. I wasn't interested in understanding her point of view. I didn't want to look at things in a different way. I wanted my own way. I was being prideful. In all honesty, I was being a knucklehead.

We had walked less than a mile, going nowhere in our conversation, when my knee suddenly gave out. There was no warning. I just took a step, and bam! I experienced excruciating pain and crumpled to the ground. Next thing I knew, I was on the ground, crying in pain. I couldn't even get up to hobble back home. So my wife left me sprawled on a stranger's lawn while she went to get the car.

While I was waiting for Charlene, expecting the homeowner to come out at any moment to say, "Hey, what are you doing on my lawn!?" God had a conversation with me. I kid you not—this really happened. I sensed God say to me:

"What'd I tell you to do?"

"I'm doing it!" I replied.

"NO YOU"RE NOT! You're being just as stubborn as you were before. I'm going to give you one chance to get this right."

"So, what do you want me to do?"

Then, God said clear as day, "Go home and read Proverbs 17:1."

"What?"

"You heard me, read Proverbs 17:1."

Charlene then returned and managed to get me back home where, still in great pain, I plopped onto the couch. While Charlene went to get an ice pack and pain reliever, I opened my Bible to Proverbs 17:1 and read, "Better a dry crust eaten in peace than a house filled with feasting—and conflict."

I started crying. I thought to myself: "I'm causing the conflict. I'm being a knucklehead. I'm running my mouth with a bad attitude. I've got to change. I've got to figure out how to pursue peace in my family."

When Charlene came back, I immediately repented. "I'm sorry," I told her. "I blew it. This disagreement is my fault. Forgive me for not listening to you." The moment I asked her to forgive me, my knee stopped hurting. I'm not kidding. I have never had anything like this happen to me before or since. But as soon as I made peace with my wife, my knee was fine. I was able to get up and walk around as if nothing had ever happened. God got His point across to me, and I hope I never forget the lesson.

Pursuing Peace

To avoid anger, we need to pursue peace, which includes pursuing peace with people we may have angered. Much has been written about how to resolve conflict, and you can easily find great resources at the library or on the internet. So I'll just summarize some basics to get you started in making peace with others.

- Swallow your pride.
- Realize there can be more than one perspective.
- Respect the other person as someone created in God's image.
- Listen to their point of view, ask questions and show interest.
- Make sure you understand their point of view. Repeat back, in your own words, what you heard the other person say.
- Look for the positives in their point of view.
- Seek to understand why they feel the way they feel. What makes them angry? Why does it make them angry?
- Avoid words that cast blame or are accusatory, angry, or would push another person's "buttons".

- Express your own views and feelings, but instead of saying "you should...," or "you ought...," use words like, "I desire...," or "as I see it...." This way you let other people know what you are thinking and feeling without telling them how they should think or feel. No one likes to be told how to think.

- You don't need to apologize for having a viewpoint, but you may need to apologize if you expressed that viewpoint in a hurtful way.

- You "win" when you make peace, not when you get your own way. Making peace means coming to a solution that both parties feel good about, and both can walk away without lingering bad feelings.

When you are soul'd out to Jesus, and your focus is on living without anger, these steps will become easier to practice. They will be things you want to do. However, there may be times where the other person will reject your efforts to make peace. Paul teaches us, "Do all that you can to live in peace with everyone" (Romans 12:18). You have no control over how another person will respond. If after doing "all that *you can*" your efforts are rejected, pray for a softening of the other's heart and leave it in God's hands.

Be a Peacemaker not just a Peacekeeper

I think it's important to point out that there is a difference between being a peacemaker and being a peacekeeper. A peacemaker is someone who actively pursues peace in their relationships. They take an active role to make peace. A peacekeeper, on the other hand, just maintains a ceasefire between two sides that are not at peace. In order to "keep" the so-called peace, peacekeepers end up not saying things that need to be said or doing things that need to be done.

Peacemaking is not for cowards. It's not for people who avoid saying things because they don't want to stir up conflict. A peacemaker will get involved in the situation. Peacemakers will "make" peace.

When you walk into a room, do people take courage or do they take cover?

They take action because they know that if they don't, they will never experience peace.

Decide to Avoid Anger

I have a question for you: When you walk into a room, do people take courage or do they take cover?

A person of character will create an atmosphere of encouragement, not fear. That's why one of the most important character decisions you can make is the decision to resist anger.

When you make that decision, and manage it the rest of your life, you'll experience a blessed life. People will be attracted to you rather than scared of you. Your life will be at peace instead of in constant turmoil. And your presence will bring peace to your home, friendships, workplace, church and neighborhood.

A Final Thought: When Anger can't be Avoided

The Bible is not naïve about the reality of anger. Ephesians 4:26-27 says, "'Don't sin by letting anger control you.' Don't let the sun go down while you are still angry, for anger gives a foothold to the devil."

Please hear me clearly on this—anger is not a sin. As I have said already, anger can be justified. Sin occurs when we let anger control us. Allowing anger to remain in our life is like building a sandbox for the devil to play in.

So when anger can't be avoided, what can you do? How can you let go of your anger before the devil gains a "foothold" in your life and destroys everything you value? In the next chapter we are going to answer these questions and discover how to use God's power to release our anger.

Decide to Forgive

"To forgive is to set a prisoner free
and discover that the prisoner was you."
- Lewis B. Smedes

Sunday dinners were a Carthen family tradition. Every Sunday
after church, all my siblings would gather at our parent's home for
dinner. I'm not talking about a simple meal of burgers or pizza. No,
we had meatloaf, fried chicken, pork chops, collard greens, yams—a
soul food feast.

We had just finished stuffing ourselves at one of these family feasts
when the phone rang. It was my father-in-law calling for Renea, my
wife at the time. He was rattled. He said that there'd been an accident
involving my wife's sister, and her kids. He asked if we could hurry to
the hospital.

My wife's sister, Diane, was a single mom who had three delightful children—a second grader, preschooler and toddler—that all of us adored. But with three young kids, life was a struggle for Diane. We were all concerned

Forgetting how uncomfortably stuffed we were from dinner, we immediately headed for the hospital. A social worker was waiting for us when we arrived and ushered us into a private room.

"There's no easy way to tell you what I have to say," she said, "so I'm just going to say it. Diane has burns to 30% of her body, but she's going to recover. Her children, however, are all dead."

The next few moments were surreal. Renea and her younger sister were screaming, and my father-in-law collapsed to the floor. I was in a haze trying to figure out if I really heard the social worker right. Did she say that my precious nieces and nephew were dead? It couldn't be true.

But as the story unfolded, we learned that my sister-in-law had snapped and lost her mind. After stabbing her children multiple times, she set the apartment on fire. She told police that a man broke into her apartment, told her to kill her children in order to save her own life, and then forced her to set the apartment on fire. However, the facts didn't support the story.

As the social worker spoke, her words barely registered with me. It was too painful. How could my nieces and nephew be dead? How could my sister-in-law be the murderer? I was numb. Then God broke through my haze and clearly asked me: "Are you going to forgive her?"

"What?!," I thought. "Are you kidding?"

"Are you going to forgive her?"

"No!"

The question came again, "Are you going to forgive her?"

This time I equivocated, "I don't know."

The truth was, I didn't want to forgive her. If everything I had just been told was true, I wanted my sister-in-law to feel the pain my nieces and nephew must have experienced. Under the numbness of my shock and disbelief, I was growing angry.

But God's question kept pressing in on me.

"Are you going to forgive?"

When Anger Cannot be Avoided

Anger, as I shared in the last chapter, can make a mess out of life. When you hold on to anger, it will destroy everything that is important to you. But what happens when anger cannot be avoided? What happens when someone does you great harm? What do you do, for instance, when you find out that innocent, young children have been murdered? What do you do with your anger in a situation like that?

The Bible is realistic about the reality of anger, but it is also clear about the necessity of letting it go. Ephesians 4:26-27 says, "'Don't sin by letting anger control you.' Don't let the sun go down while you are still angry, for anger gives a foothold to the devil." Notice that this passage recognizes the reality of anger. Further, it does not call anger a sin. The sin, according to these verses, is when we hang on to the anger and allow it to take control. When anger takes control, we end up doing things that are sinful and destructive. You know I'm telling the truth because you've been there and done that, just as I have. Can I say, "Amen, all by myself?"

Although there are times when anger can't be avoided, we simply cannot continue to hold on to that anger. For the sake of our health, our relationships, and the very quality of our lives, we need to learn how to let it go before it destroys us.

The good news is: God gives us clear and effective instructions on how to let go of anger. The hard part isn't learning what to do with our anger. We can find that in the Bible. The hard part is being willing to act on what the Bible teaches. Can I get a witness here?

The Only Solution

So how do we let go of anger? The Bible says simply that we need to forgive. This is not my idea, it is God's. I know for some of you right now, just the thought of forgiving someone who has harmed you is making you angry. In fact, you may want to slam this book shut right now. Don't do it! If you shut this book now, you'll miss out on all that God has for you. So keep on reading. Give me a chance to make my case. Then decide whether or not I'm out of my mind.

In Matthew 6, Jesus' disciples asked him for instruction on how to pray. In response, Jesus taught them the Lord's Prayer. It is a surprisingly short and simple prayer, just a statement of praise followed by four quick requests. Since it is Jesus doing the teaching, I have to assume He considers these four requests to be some of the most important things we could ever pray for. One of those four requests is: "Forgive us our sins, as *we forgive* those who have sinned against us" (Matthew 6:12, *emphasis mine*).

Forgiveness is a big deal to Jesus. It's on his Top Four list of things we should pray about. But we don't seem to share Jesus' enthusiasm. You won't find a line at the Forgiveness Store that goes out the door and around the corner, where people are excitedly saying, "I'm here to get me a can of forgiveness. I hope they don't run out."

In our society, when you forgive, you're seen as being weak, a wimp, a punk. Forgiveness is not attractive to us.

It is revenge that's glamorous, not forgiveness. Revenge is what sells tickets to the movies. The hero of the story is the person who

> *When you forgive, you're seen as being weak, a wimp, a punk. Forgiveness is not attractive.*

gets even. We cheer for the person who settles the score.

However, forgiveness is God's only plan for saving the world. There is no second option. There is no "Plan B." Jesus said plainly that his mission was to find and save the lost (Luke 19:10). Elsewhere, He said that He came so we can "have life, and have it to the full" (John 10:10, NIV). Jesus went to the cross to accomplish that mission.

To send Jesus to the cross, his opponents had to first trump up bogus charges against him. Then, after he was sentenced, they beat him to a bloody pulp, pressed a crown of thorns into his forehead, forced him to carry the heavy wooden beams of his own cross and then nailed him to that cross. If I were preaching this at my own church I would say, "They kicked his butt up one wall and down the other!"

But after experiencing all of that, Jesus had the nerve, the gall, the audacity to say, "Father, *forgive* them for they do not know what they are doing" (Luke 23:24, *emphasis mine*).

I don't mean any harm. Please hear me. *There was no other plan!* There was no other way. Forgiveness was, and still is, the only solution.

> I don't mean any harm, but forgiveness was, and is, God's only solution.

We do not even need the Bible to help us recognize that forgiveness is the only solution. Politicians have worked for decades to bring peace to the Middle East, but in all honesty all they're really trying to accomplish is a ceasefire. There cannot be peace in the Middle East without forgiveness. It is the only solution.

Going further, there cannot be peace between whites and blacks, whites and browns, and browns and blacks without forgiveness. There cannot be peace between a mom and her daughter, a father and his son, or a husband and wife without forgiveness. Forgiveness is the only solution. Do you hear what I'm saying?

So why do we prefer revenge?

When we seek revenge, we only escalate the hostility and make things worse. As Gandhi once said, "If we all lived by 'an eye for an eye,' then the whole world would be blind." And maybe that's the problem, maybe we've all been blinded by our anger.

The Power of Forgiveness

You may not realize this, but when you follow God's plan and forgive, you unleash God's power in your life. God works through your act of forgiveness to remove your anger, and He replaces it with peace and joy. I've seen this countless times in my own life and in the lives of others. For example:

A man was bitter after his wife left him. He walked around bristling with anger. People would rather take their chances with a porcupine than go near him. Finally, he came to the point of saying, "This has to stop. I'm making myself and everyone around me miserable." He used the prayer I will share with you later in this chapter to forgive his ex-wife, and he was transformed. Now, everyone wants to be around him.

A dad was angry over losing his job and was taking his anger out on his kids. The kids responded by becoming increasingly belligerent and rebellious. It was just a matter of time before their rebelliousness got them into the kind of trouble that would have permanent consequences. Barely in time, dad decided to forgive the people who had sacked him. As a result, his demeanor changed, the way he treated his kids changed, and his kids changed as well. His family was saved from destruction.

A marriage was on the rocks. But instead of tumbling into the abyss, they put their trust in the solid Rock. The couple followed God's plan and forgave each other. Their love began to blossom and now their marriage is solid as a rock.

I have seen scenarios like these played out time and time again. It's thrilling to see the miracles God does in a life, and a family, when we trust His plan. But sadly, I've also seen it go the other way. I have seen lives, marriages and families torn apart and destroyed because people refused to forgive.

How do We do It?

But what does forgiveness look like? How do we do it?

We all have a vague sense of what forgiveness is, but honestly, most of what passes for forgiveness is shallow. Because forgiveness is not valued in our society, there are few examples of real

Most of what passes as forgiveness is shallow and doesn't result in powerful life-change.

forgiveness for us to follow. What we try to pass off as forgiveness lacks substance and doesn't result in the kind of powerful life-change I've been talking about.

I've been looking around, but I don't see many places where forgiveness is being taught. Where can you go to take a class on forgiveness? Where are the seminars on developing forgiveness skills? You don't see forgiveness taught as part of a leadership course. Nor do you hear politicians talking about forgiveness (they're too busy trying to draw attention to themselves by getting in a clever "shot" at their opponents).

A school district near me has started using a "values-based" curriculum because they recognize the importance of developing moral character in their students. I was curious, so I checked out their materials. There were some outstanding character traits being incorporated into the curriculum, but forgiveness wasn't included. Amazing! We are truly the blind leading the blind.

Even in church we rarely teach people how to forgive. We also do a terrible job of practicing forgiveness, which leads cynics to comment that "Christians are the only people who shoot their wounded." I grew up in a church that said the Lord's Prayer every Sunday, not just once, but twice and sometimes even three times a service. But no matter how many times we prayed, "Forgive us our sins as we forgive those who have sinned against us," I cannot remember anyone saying: "This is what forgiveness looks like. This is how you offer forgiveness when you get hurt, wounded, or offended."

We weren't even good at modeling forgiveness at home. Although I grew up in a God-fearing, church-going family, forgiveness was not one of our strengths. I watched family members, myself included, hold on to grudges and then wait for a strategic moment when we could rehash the dirty laundry and make the other person look bad.

Truth is we live in a forgiveness-challenged world. We have had too little teaching and too few models on forgiveness. As a result, you may not have a clear understanding of what real forgiveness is or how to practice it.

Forgiveness Comes from the Heart

Let me ask you, have you ever thought that you had forgiven someone, but then every time you think about that person you get angry? That's a sure sign that your forgiveness was shallow and missed the mark.

Forgiveness is not the shallow, blanket statement of "I forgive you" that we often say with little sincerity. Jesus teaches us that forgiveness, the kind that taps into God's power and removes anger, needs to come from down deep. It needs to come from the heart (Matthew 18:35). Here is my recipe for forgiving from your heart.

A Recipe for Forgiveness

Step 1: Identify the Offense

The first step we must take to forgive from the heart is to identify the specific offenses we are forgiving. I think people really struggle with getting specific, at least I have. Many times people will say, "Well, you're forgiven." Forgiven for what? This wide brush of forgiveness will not work because it does not dig down to the source of the pain.

To truly forgive, you need to identify the offense. What was it that was said or done that has hurt you? You were hurt by specific acts done by specific people. It is those specific acts that need to be forgiven. If you don't identify and forgive specific acts, the wounds they cause will not be healed, and they will continue to hurt you again and again.

Step 2: Own the Pain

Forgiving from the heart also means owning the pain. If you can identify the offense, then you can own the pain. There are too many people who will say, "It's okay. It's alright. I'm good."

Stop lying! I know you think that you're being tough, or that you are being gracious. I know that you don't want to show weakness. But you're not doing yourself any favors. You have been hurt! You need to own the pain so that you can be released from it.

The heart is where our feelings and emotions lie. So, to forgive from the heart you need to get in touch with the feelings and emotions caused by the offense. You need to say something like: "When they did _____, I felt _____ (betrayed, abused, depressed, rejected, worthless, humiliated, angry, etc.)." What is it you feel? If you don't own your hurt and pain, you're walking in deception. You will not be able to forgive from your heart.

When you deny your pain, all you're doing is covering up the offense. It's like sweeping dirt under the carpet or putting makeup over the blemish. But the wound is still there. And when you least expect it somebody is going to lift the carpet, or the makeup is going to wash away and the ugliness will be revealed.

You cannot hide from your hurt and pain. If you try, you'll just make a mess of your life. Again let me say, "Amen, all by myself," because I have tried to hide the hurt and it only messed me up. In order to be free of the anger and pain of an offense, you have to bring the feelings out of hiding and own them.

Step 3: Decide to let Go

Once you have identified the offense and owned the feelings, you are ready to forgive and let go of the hurt. But the decision to forgive is a hard one to make. When we decide to forgive a person who has hurt us, that person no longer owes us anything! We have forgiven the debt.

This is very hard to do because it is human nature to say, "I want you to feel what I feel. I want to even the score." But when you decide to forgive, there's no longer any score to settle.

Forgiveness is a challenge for me because it doesn't seem fair. When I'm hurt or offended, I want the other person to feel my pain. I'm not proud of that, but I need to be real with you. I seldom feel like forgiving. That is why we must *decide* to forgive, because if we wait until we feel like forgiving we will seldom do it.

But the decision to forgive is not an easy one to make. Even as I write this I am struggling to come to the point of being willing to forgive someone who has hurt me. I can picture God smiling right now at the irony of my situation. I must make a choice about whether or not I will forgive this person. Honestly, this choice is a hard one.

However, I've never regretted forgiving. Although deciding to forgive was hard, once I made the decision I've always been glad.

Get off the Hook

I want to share with you some things that have helped me make the decision to forgive. We often look at forgiveness in terms of what it means for the offender. Forgiving would mean letting the offender off the hook, and when you look at it from that angle, why would you want to do that?

However, when you shift your focus away from what happens to the offender and onto what happens to yourself, things look different. When you withhold forgiveness, you hold onto the wound and its pain. You stay stuck on the hook of the person who hurt you. However, when you forgive, God heals the wound and removes the pain. When you look at it from this angle you realize that through forgiveness you take yourself off the hook—and why wouldn't you want to do that?

Enter the Flow of God's Power

For me, there is an even more compelling reason to choose to forgive: when you forgive, God's life-changing power is released in your life. You enter into the flow of God's work when you forgive, and as a result you experience the blessings of His presence. However, if you refuse

When you forgive, God's life-changing power is released in your life.

to forgive, you reject God's plan and deprive yourself of the life He wants to pour into you.

Jesus taught a story about forgiveness in Matthew 18 that kicks my butt every time I read it. The story is about a guy who didn't get it. He was a servant who owed his master hundreds of thousands of dollars, a debt that was as impossible for him to repay as it would be for me. In those days, when you couldn't repay a debt, not only was your home repossessed, your family was sold into slavery. If that still wasn't enough to cover the debt, you were put into prison until the debt was paid off. Since it's hard to earn money in prison, being sent there to pay off a debt could mean a life sentence. Can you imagine what this would do to credit card companies if this were our practice today?

In a panic, this debtor pleaded with his master for more time to pay off the debt. The master, knowing that the debt was too large to ever be covered, did more than give the servant more time. The master forgave the debt entirely. The servant walked out of the master's office free and clear of hundreds of thousands of dollars in debt.

On the way out of the Master's office, the servant ran into a co-worker who owed him a few hundred dollars. The servant grabbed his coworker by the throat and demand that he pay back his debt immediately. The coworker didn't have the money and fell to his knees begging for a little more time. However, as his very first act as a forgiven man, the servant threw his coworker into prison. This servant didn't get it. He had no appreciation for the enormity of the forgiveness he had just experienced.

Jesus finishes the story by saying that when the master found out about what had been done, he was enraged. He called the servant back in, reversed his decision, and "in anger...handed him over to the jailers to be tortured, until he should pay back all he owed."

Jesus then drove home the point of the story with one sentence. "This is how my heavenly Father will treat each of you unless you forgive your brother or sister from your heart" (Matthew 18:35).

Good God Almighty, that's scary. The servant didn't get it. Do you?

God has forgiven us a debt of sin we could never repay. Our willingness or unwillingness to forgive others will show how much we understand and appreciate this great gift God has given us.

To withhold forgiveness is to reject the forgiveness God has offered you. That is something I never want to do. I would much rather be in the flow of God's power, allowing him to remove my anger and then fill me with His joy and peace. What about you?

Offering Forgiveness

Once you decide to forgive, the act of forgiveness is easy. You start by forgiving the person before God through a simple yet effective prayer that identifies the offense and owns the emotions. The prayer will go something like this:

> Dear Jesus,
> I choose to forgive *(name of person)*, for doing *(specific action that hurt you)*, and causing me to feel *(the feelings you felt)*.
> Amen.

That is a prayer of forgiveness that comes from the heart. When you pray this prayer, God will begin a work of transformation that will heal your wound and remove its sting.

I should point out here that forgiveness is not contingent on the other party admitting wrong-doing or asking for forgiveness. If you wait on them, you stay on their hook. Forgiveness is your decision and something you can do before God. That's the first step. Reconciliation—if possible—is the next step.

If you are given the opportunity, forgiving someone face-to-face is very similar to forgiving someone before God. In my experience, you need to talk with the person about the actions that hurt you and how it made you feel. If you don't talk about those things, your forgiveness will be shallow. You need to bring up the pain in order to let God heal the wound. You must deal with it.

Forgiveness Doesn't Equal Trust

Sometimes we withhold forgiveness because we mistakenly believe that it means we must now trust that person, but there is a difference between forgiveness and trust. When we forgive a person, it means we will no longer hold a grudge against them or seek to even the score. The debt they owed us is settled.

However, forgiveness does not mean we must trust them. Our forgiveness does not make a person trustworthy. Forgiveness is a gift we give, but trust must be earned.

Forgiveness allows you to once again love the other person as a child of God, and it opens up the possibility of a restored relationship. But forgiveness doesn't take you back in time to pick up things where they were left. Forgiveness unties you from the past so that you can move forward. By God's grace, a new relationship can possibly form.

But relationships and trust can only be built, or rebuilt, over time and they may be different from what they were in the past—and that's okay.

Will You Forgive?

When I talk about forgiveness, people who don't know my past will say, "Sherwood that's easy for you to say. You're a preacher; you're supposed to say that." They don't get it. They don't know what I've experienced. Forgiveness is not easy for me to talk about. I'm not proud of this, but I did not want to forgive my sister-in-law for murdering her children.

I'm not going to fake the funk with you. When God asked me if I would forgive my sister-in-law, forgiveness was the last thing I wanted to do. I wanted to hold my sister-in-law's actions against her. But what good would that have done? It wouldn't have changed anything. It wouldn't even make me feel better. I would just be hurting myself and the work God wanted to do in me.

I remember sensing God say, "If you don't forgive her, you'll never treat her right, and worse, she may never experience my love." So in that moment, I chose to forgive.

When I forgave my sister-in-law, it didn't take away my memories of that tragedy. I still feel sadness whenever I think about it. Matter of fact, I'm reaching for the Kleenex now. But I no longer feel angry or bitter.

I did not want to forgive the person who molested me either. But the anger I felt because of that trauma was making a mess of my life and threatening to destroy my future. I finally got to the point of saying, "I'm done feeling like this. I'm tired of being hurt and wounded. I'm tired of thinking up ways to retaliate. I'm ready to give up this pain so I can live." That is when I chose to forgive.

"I'm tired of being hurt... I'm ready to give up this pain." That's when I chose to forgive.

Once I forgave my molester, God miraculously healed my wound. Again, the memory is still there, but the sting of the memory is gone—so is the anger that was destroying my life.

Now God is able to work through me to give hope and healing to others who have gone through similar experiences. I'm in the flow of God's power.

A Decision to Last a Lifetime

During the civil rights movement, African-Americans were being beaten with clubs, attacked by dogs, and hosed with the full force of fire hoses. Their homes were fire-bombed, and some people were even murdered. During the height of all this suffering, Martin Luther King Jr. preached forgiveness, knowing that it was the only solution. He told people that, "Forgiveness is not an occasional act. It is a *permanent attitude*" (Italics mine).

Forgiveness must become a "permanent attitude" in us, part of our character, who we are at the core. We must decide to forgive, not just once and awhile, not just when we feel like it, not only when someone has earned our forgiveness. We must decide to forgive—period. When we decide to forgive, it will set us free from the past. But forgiving past offenses is only the beginning. We need to continue forgiving whenever we are wronged. If we start to pick and choose who we forgive and who we won't forgive, we will only hurt ourselves. We will allow unforgiven wounds to have destructive power in our lives, and we will be stepping out of the flow of God's power.

When you come to a settled decision that you will be a forgiving person, you'll be equipped to forgive whenever you are hurt, and anchored when angry emotions threaten to overwhelm you and lead you to do things that would cause greater harm. Because of your decision, God's character will grow stronger in you, and you will become a man or woman who will make your marriage, family, friendships, and the world around you better.

Do You Get It?

Chances are, as you read this chapter, you thought of someone you need to forgive. That is God speaking to you. He is pointing out the wounds He wants to heal. Do you believe that He will release His power in you when you forgive? Will you trust God and be soul'd out to His forgiveness plan?

God is asking, "Do you get it? Will you forgive?"

When you do, God will take the misery from your memory. So, forgive and be healed in Jesus' name. Amen.

Decide to be Content

"I have learned the secret of being content in any and every situation."
- the Apostle Paul

I was speaking at a special event when I first met "Joe". He came up to me afterwards and introduced himself and his wife. He was a businessman, but was exploring the possibility of a midlife career change to go "into the ministry." We had a great conversation, and then stayed in touch afterwards. Soon he and his wife began attending the church where I served as pastor. I enjoyed his company, and over time I became a sounding board for him.

In order to help him explore a ministry career, I would often bring him along on different ministry outings. At one point, Joe came with me to an overnight speaking engagement a few hours from my home. While I was driving, Joe said, "Hey, let me get your take on something."

Then he began to share with me how discontented he was with his life. He was discontented with his marriage, discontented with his job, and discontented with what he had accomplished and not accomplished. He was discontented with just about everything, to the point that he had decided to quit his job and his marriage and restart his life. He had come to the conclusion that starting over was the only solution to finding the contentment that eluded him. "So," he asked, "what do you think?"

As a concerned friend, I tried to speak wise counsel into his life. But it became apparent that no matter what I said, or how much biblical wisdom I shared, it wasn't going to make any difference. He didn't really want my views, he wanted my approval. When I failed to support his decisions, he got upset. From his perspective, I was failing to understand how horrible his situation was. "If you could live my life," he said, "this would all make sense to you."

Joe was riding the rails of discontentment, and I was unable to de-rail the train. In short order he left the church, had an affair that destroyed two marriages, and lost his job. I've lost contact with Joe, but I doubt he's any more content now than he was before he blew up his life.

Craving More

God warns us through His word not to "love this world nor the things it offers you, for when you love the world, you do not have the love of the Father in you. For the world offers only a craving for physical pleasure, a craving for everything we see, and pride in our achievements and possessions. These are not from the Father, but are from this world. And this world is fading away, along with everything that people crave. But anyone who does what pleases God will live forever" (1 John 2:15-17).

My friend Joe is proof positive that God knows what He's talking about. Joe's cravings for more led him to destroy all the blessings he already enjoyed—and he's not alone. I see it in the community I live in, the society I belong to, the nation I am a citizen of—people are never content. Did you hear what I said? We are never satisfied. We never have enough. No matter how little or how much we have, we always crave more. And it's destroying us.

We are never satisfied. We never have enough. And it's destroying us.

Our world is struggling economically right now because people wanted more. It didn't matter if they couldn't pay for it right away, because they could borrow and pay for it later. So people kept borrowing and buying until they borrowed beyond their ability to pay it back.

Want another example of not being satisfied? America has the embarrassing distinction of being the "fattest" country in the world. We eat beyond what's healthy, yet we keep craving more. I'm not proud of this, but I have to admit that I have done my share to contribute to this problem.

We always want something bigger or better than what we already have, whether it's even bigger screen TVs, fancier homes, faster cars, newer gadgets, or sexier relationships. However, in my observation, rather than bringing us success, our cravings lead to our ruin. If we want to be people who achieve our God-given potential, we must make some crucial decisions that will break us of the cravings that are destroying us.

The Lust of the Flesh

The first craving mentioned in 1 John 2:15-17 is the craving for physical pleasures, also called the "lust of the flesh" in other translations of the Bible. This craving can show up in our lives in a variety ways. For some people, it's all about their looks. They pursue the perfect body, the perfect hair, the perfect shape. They invest inordinate amounts of time and money on cosmetics, exercise, hair styles, clothing, surgeries, gimmicks, gadgets, and supplements.

For other people, it's food they crave. They love to eat and eat and eat. "That tasted so good," they say, "I just have to have a little more." Soon their bodies get so used to consuming large quantities of food that it doesn't even matter whether or not they're hungry, they eat because they're bodies crave more food.

In other cases, it's all about sex. They don't just want it, they crave it. They can never have enough. I know what you're thinking. You're thinking, "That's just called being a man." I assure you, this is not true.

I know of a man who wanted to lose a significant amount of weight. His wife, wanting to encourage him, told him that he could look forward to sex every night for a month once he reached his goal.

Not surprisingly, the husband lost the weight in record time (he is a man after all). True to her word, the couple started having sex every night. He hung in there for two weeks before he finally had to admit to his wife that he couldn't go on another night. He was exhausted (so was she). Too much of a good thing can become a bad thing.

Just like any craving, a craving for sexual pleasure that knows no boundaries will become destructive and lead to abuse, affairs and addiction to pornography. It will soon dominate, and then ruin, healthy relationships.

For still other people, their craving is for physical activity. These people don't just *like* to play golf, they *love* to play golf and play it every moment they can. Or it could be basketball, tennis, or any other physical activity. Their craving takes over their time, attention and wallet.

Finally there are drugs and alcohol that offer people a "high". However, after they've had a "high" they want to go higher. They crave more, and soon they are trapped in an addiction.

Just to be clear, I'm not saying that enjoying food is bad, or that you shouldn't care about your appearance, or that sex is evil. Illegal drugs are bad, but the other things—food, exercise, recreation, and sex—are all given by God for our health and enjoyment. The danger comes when we develop cravings for these things. When we are never satisfied, the things God gives to make our lives enjoyable end up controlling us, and then destroying us.

Craving God

So how do we protect ourselves from destructive cravings for physical pleasure? I believe the answer is given in Paul's advice to Timothy. Paul warns that people who always want more end up plunging themselves into "ruin and destruction," and pierce themselves with "many sorrows" (1 Timothy 6:9-10). To combat this trap, Paul tells Timothy that "godliness with *contentment* is great gain" (1 Timothy 6:6, NIV, *emphasis mine*).

According to this verse, there are two decisions to be made here. The first decision is to be godly. To be godly is to be soul'd out to obeying God in everything—it means craving God. John warned us not to "love this world nor the things it offers you, for when you love the world, you do not have the love of the Father in you. For the world offers only a craving for physical pleasure...."

Because we are God's creation, only God's presence and love can truly fill our lives. Jesus tells us that only He is the one who can fill *Because the "love of the Father" is missing...we try to fill the void...with all the wrong things.* us and give us "life to the full" (John 10:10). Without God's presence, we can never feel full, we can never feel fulfilled.

We develop cravings because the "love of the Father" is missing from our lives. So we try to fill the void. But we do it with all the wrong things.

Instead of filling the void with God's love, we try to fill it with physical pleasure, material things, or a driven need for power and self-importance. But they all come up short. These things will never bring satisfaction, because the void in our lives cannot be filled with physical things. The void can only be filled with God's presence and love. What we need to do is crave God, not physical pleasures.

Choosing Contentment

After the decision to be godly, the second decision that will help us combat cravings for physical pleasure is to decide to be content. When Paul says that "godliness with contentment is great gain," he is not just spouting off pious platitudes that are based on wishful thinking. He's speaking from his own experience.

While imprisoned in Rome, Paul wrote to the church in Philippi that he had"learned to be content whatever the circumstances. I know what it is to be in need, and I know what it is to have plenty. I have learned the secret of being content in any and every situation, whether well fed or hungry, whether living in plenty or in want. I can do all this through him who gives me strength" (Philippians 4:11-13, NIV).

Contentment means being satisfied with what you have. Whether you have a lot or a little, you're satisfied. Whether you live on an estate or in a cramped apartment, you're comfortable. Whether your closet is filled with the latest fashions from Nordstrom or well-worn clothes from Wal-Mart, you're at ease. Contentment is the opposite of craving.

However, when we are discontent we are more likely to argue and blame others. When we are discontent we are miserable and make everyone around us miserable. When we are discontent we end up doing the stupid—like my friend Joe—and it blows up in our faces. Discontentment robs us of peace, but when we are content, we will find peace.

Contentment is also the absence of stress and frustration. When we crave things, we are always dissatisfied, always disappointed, and always driven as we strive for more. This discontentment and driven-ness create frustration and stress. On the other hand, when we are content with what we have, stress and frustration are reduced, if not eliminated.

I am certain that you do not want to live with frustration, stress and tension in your life. But to change your life you must learn what Paul calls "the secret of being content in any and every situation."

The Secret to Being Content

First, let me point out what is obvious to those who know me. I have a long way to go in the area of learning to be content. I have my good moments when I'm at peace, regardless of circumstances. I also have my bad moments, and in those moments I've come close to making some terrible decisions.

In my career as a pastor, I have almost resigned six times. I've gone as far as writing the resignation letter, because I was dissatisfied with how things were going. Of course, I felt "the church" was the cause of my discontentment (after all, it couldn't be me). I was sure that once I quit, I'd be content. That's six times I almost destroyed the work God wanted to do in me and through me. Fortunately, God got my attention and mercifully prevented me from blowing myself up and taking innocent bystanders with me.

God has been teaching me a lot about contentment, and as I have listened and learned, He has brought more contentment into my life. I'm not a contentment expert, but as a partner with you on this journey, let me share three rock-solid truths I've learned that have helped me learn to be content.

1. Know that God is in control.
2. Trust that God is for you.
3. Yield to God completely.

God is in Control

In this life, people will use the difficulties they have faced to justify their cravings. I know guys who, because of rough childhoods, brought pain, anger and anxiety into their adult lives. In order to cope, they turned to drugs. "I need the marijuana to settle me down," one guy told me, "otherwise I'd never make it through the day." Other guys turned to crack cocaine to forget about their pain and to escape the pressures of life.

These guys thought, "If there is a God, and He let these bad things happen to me, then He must not be in control." So to make it in life, these guys eliminated God from the equation and took matters into their own hands. But instead of gaining control of their lives, they lost control to their addictions. Things didn't go well for them. Some of these guys gave up in despair, left their wives and kids, and simply disappeared. Others lost their jobs. Many lost their families because their wives wouldn't put up with their addictions.

Drugs or alcohol aren't the only things that people turn to when they are discontent. Some people turn to affairs, some to thrill seeking, some to shopping, and some to workaholism. The list of things people turn to in an effort to take control of their lives and feel alive is nearly endless. But these things all have one thing in common. They all produce cravings, but never satisfaction. They do not provide "the secret to being content in any and every situation."

To live a life of contentment, we must get to a place where we know beyond a shadow of a doubt that God is in control. I know a lot of folks who like to say, "God is in control," but I'm not sure that they have thought through all the implications. When you say God is in control, you are saying that nothing in this life happens unless it first passes across the desk of God. God is aware of everything that is going to happen to you, and nothing happens to you without His approval.

I know folks who like to say, 'God is in control,' but I'm not sure they thought through the implications.

This is going to be a struggle for a lot of folks, because it means that the most damnable things that have happened in your life first passed God's desk before it got to you. I know that's not a happy thought, but let me go to the Bible to back up what I'm saying. Lamentations 3:37-38 says, "Who can command things to happen without the Lord's permission? Does not the Most High send both calamity and good?"

For reasons sometimes known only to Him, God has signed off on the worst tragedies you have experienced. When I was molested as a child, God allowed it to happen. God allowed my nieces and nephew to be murdered. And God is well aware of whatever pain you are experiencing right now. These are challenging implications of God being in control. These are implications that make people mad, or worse, cause them to reject God—because if God really is in control why doesn't He stop these things from happening?

It is not my intention here to get into a theological discussion about the problem of evil and the role of free will. These things have been covered well by others. (see endnote)* My focus here is to help us get to a place of contentment, and contentment requires a certainty that God is in control.

Think this through with me. If you don't believe that God is in control of even the tragedies of life, then that means there are things that happen that God has no control over. It means that the devil can actually defeat God—the devil can do stuff and God can't stop Him. If God is not in control, it means there is a force, a circumstance, a situation that is out of His control. If that's the case, we'll never be content because we'll always be craving for something that can provide protection.

If you don't believe God is in control, then you are going to try to fix your situation on your own. You're going to seek a solution that doesn't involve God, and you'll end up doing something that will mess you up. Then, ironically, you will be mad at God and say, "This just proves once again that God is not in control." Proverbs 19:3 says, "People ruin their lives by their own foolishness and then they are angry at the Lord."

People ask me, "Sherwood, after all that has happened to you, why do you still believe that God is in control?" I always point them to Psalms 11:3-4, which says, "'The foundations of law and order have collapsed. What can the righteous do?' But the LORD is in his holy Temple; the LORD still rules from heaven." In my mind, that verse settles it for me. Even if the social order around us is collapsing, God is still in control!

If we want to reach a place where we are no longer controlled by cravings and discontentment, we need to come to the conclusion that no matter how bad things are, no matter how unwanted our circumstances, God is still in control.

God Is For Me

To know that God is in control is not enough to live a life of contentment. We also need to trust that God is for us. This was part of the Apostle Paul's secret to contentment. In Romans 8:31 Paul writes, "If God is for us, who can ever be against us?"

What's stunning about this verse is that Paul is writing to believers in Rome who are dealing with persecution. Rome was trying to take over the world, and Christianity was seen as a threat to their power.

People who had just put their faith in Jesus Christ were being pulled out of their homes and told to denounce Christ or lose their lives. To them, it felt like the whole world was against them. It is to these folks that Paul dares to say, "If God is for us, who can ever be against us?" Paul is telling these beleaguered Christians, "Remember, no matter what you go through, be content, because God is for you."

However, when I am struggling, it can be easy for me to forget that God is for me. I don't know why, but sometimes I forget that God's got my back. I allow history, circumstances and even people to get me thinking that God doesn't have my best interests in mind.

Psalm 23:6 says, "Goodness and love will follow me all the days of my life" (NIV). I like to tell people that no matter where I go, I have these two friends that follow me. They show up in meetings, in struggles, even in confrontations. These two friends are goodness and love. These friends come from God, and they have my back. When I remember that goodness and love are following me, I can relax. I know everything is going to be fine. Even in dark valleys, I know it's all going to work out, because my two friends have my back.

To be content, I need to keep reminding myself that God is for me, that His goodness and love follow me. I think that's true for all of us.

Fortunately, God has gone above and beyond in his efforts to show that He is for us. Romans 5:8 says, "But God showed his great love for us by sending Christ to die for us while we were still sinners."

The cross is the ultimate sign of God being for us. When we experience pain in our life, the cross reminds us that God is not looking the other way. The cross shows us that God not only knows our pain, He shares our pain. He feels it even more acutely than we do.

But the cross is not the end of the story. The tremendous news is that there is also the promise of resurrection! Romans 6:5 gives us the good news: "If we have been united with him in a death like his, we will certainly also be united with him in a resurrection like his" (NIV).

God is for you! He thinks you're valuable enough to die for, and He offers you the promise of resurrection. When you can trust in this promise, you can be content in all circumstances.

However, when I start to doubt that God is for me, that's when I start whining about all the things others have that I don't have. I complain that "Life is not fair."

When we know God is for us we can be content. We know we'll come out okay, no matter what hits us.

This is the point where my cravings start to take control of me. I start making everything about me, and end up making everything worse. And that only increases my discontentment.

When we can trust that God is for us, we break the cycle. When we are certain that God is for us—I mean really for us—then no matter what hits our lives, we know it's going to bring us to the end God has planned—an end that will bring us fulfillment and glorify Him.

When I know God is for me, I can be content knowing that I will come out okay. I'm going to be alright. I can trust that He will take even the worst situations and turn them for my good.

Job 23:10 says, "But he knows where I am going. And when he tests me, I will come out as pure as gold." If we want to live a life of contentment, we have to settle in our minds that there is a God who is in control and trust that God is actually for us.

Yielding to God

Once you've established that you are not in control, and you can trust that God has your best interests in mind, your final step is to yield yourself to God. Proverbs 3:5-6 says, "Trust in the Lord with all your heart and lean not on your own understanding; in all your ways submit to Him and He will make your paths straight" (NIV).

I don't know about you, but I'm the kind of guy who wants to make sense out of stuff. I want to understand why God signed off on some of the painful things I experienced in my life—things that, frankly, don't make sense. In my quest to be okay with what has happened to me, I have turned to Scripture for counsel, and I've been surprised by what I've discovered. I found verse after verse where God says, "Trust me," but no verses where God says, "Understand me."

In Isaiah 55:8-9 God says, "'My thoughts are nothing like your thoughts,' says the LORD. 'My ways are far beyond anything you could imagine. For just as the heavens are higher than the earth, so my ways are higher than your ways and my thoughts higher than your thoughts.'" I've come to the realization that if God were small enough for me to understand, He wouldn't be big enough for me to trust. Amen all by myself!

Some things we'll never understand. If we want to live a life of contentment, we need to let go of our desire to understand everything that happens to us, and let God be in control. We need to get to a place where we yield to God and trust in His decisions. I'm reminded of the old hymn we sang in church when I was a boy that went, "We'll understand it better by and by."

Trust means that no matter what is going on in our lives, we know God is in control, and we will trust that He has us on the right path. Whether things are going for or against us, whether we're on top of the world or scraping bottom, whether we're full or hungry, rich or poor, healthy or sick, God says, "You need to trust me. I am in control and I know what I am doing. If you trust me, I will make sure that you are in the right place, to do the right thing, at just the right time."

When you can yield to God because you know He is in control and He is for you, you will find contentment. You will be able to trust your life to God, trust your goals and success to God, and trust your future to God. Allstate Insurance tells its customers that they can relax because they are in "good hands." Well, when you yield to God, you can truly relax because you are in God's hands. "He will never leave you or forsake you" (Deuteronomy 31:6).

Contentment vs. Complacency

Oftentimes, contentment is undervalued because it is mistaken for complacency or a lack of ambition. Complacency is an attitude that says, "I don't want to do any more. I have done enough. I have grown enough. I have served enough. I have given enough. I have achieved enough. Now, I am going to be a couch potato." Complacency is the opposite of yielding to God, who always wants to take us deeper into a relationship with Him and further in serving Him. Complacency does not bring contentment. Instead, complacency fuels cravings because it leads to a life of boredom.

Contentment also does not mean that a person is unambitious. Just because I'm content, it doesn't mean I have achieved all that I want to achieve. It doesn't mean that I lack dreams and goals. It just means that I'm where God has me today. Although I may be poor, that's only where God has me today. Check back with me next week or next year to see where God has me then.

I have dreams and goals I have not yet reached, but I am content. I'm not grumbling and complaining about my situation. I'm not frustrated that I haven't yet reached my goals. I do not blame other people because I'm not living my dream. I believe I'm where God needs me. I don't have to force the issue or get stressed out. I'm content even as I work towards my goals.

Contentment is Your Choice

You will never be a person of character and significance if you let your cravings for physical pleasure define who you are. The discontentment you feel in your life will drive you to make decisions that can destroy you and hurt those around you.

But you can make a different choice. You can decide to be content. I want to emphasize that this must be a decision. In our sinful world, contentment is not who we are by default. If you do not *decide* to be content, you'll be swept away by the powerful torrent of your cravings, and they will control you.

The secret to contentment is to decide each day that, no matter what is happening around you, God is in control and God is for you. Then, yield yourself to God. Let Him be in control. When you take these steps, God will fill you with his presence. Your cravings will be expelled from your life along with the stress and tension that comes with them, and you'll experience God's joy.

* If you would like to learn more on the topics of free will and the problem of evil, I recommend the book *Case for Faith* by Lee Strobel, published by Zondervan, or *Searching Issues* by Nicky Gumbel, available from AlphaUSA.

Decide to be Generous

"There's no good reason to be the richest man in the cemetery."
– Colonel Sanders

Congratulations!!! Odds are you are exceptional…at spending. You know how to find a bargain. You consider a mere 10% off a waste of your time. In fact, you may be so good at finding bargains that you're going broke saving money. Some of you are so exceptional that you take it to the next level and spend more than you have.

Take Jenny for example. She recently graduated from college with a $20,000 school loan. In order to look good for job interviews, she put a couple thousand dollars worth of clothes and accessories on her credit card. This was on top of the $4,000 of credit card debt she had already built up while in school, "because a girl has to have some fun." Jenny also needed a reliable car for transportation. She "saved" money by buying a used car, so her car loan was only $6,000. Fortunately, Jenny's "investments" paid off, and she was able to land a job.

If she had watched her expenses, Jenny could have paid off her debts in ten years or less, but like most of us, Jenny had a standard of living to keep up. She wanted to be able to go out with her friends, and it was important to look stylish in order to "catch the eye of the right kind of guy." Add to that an apartment to furnish, cable TV, high-speed internet... and Jenny's debt kept going up instead of down.

Jenny did catch the eye of a wonderful guy and fell in love. Bob was caring, responsible, had a good job, and he adored Jenny. They were soon engaged. Swept away by the rush of love, Jenny didn't give a thought to her financial problems. Between their two incomes, she reasoned, her minor difficulties would soon be solved.

Bob, however, had his own spending issues. He had a beautiful sports car that Jenny loved. The bank loved the car too, or at least it loved the interest it collected on the $20,000 car loan. Bob also liked having the newest and best of everything, assuming he could afford it. Unfortunately, Bob assumed he could afford anything that didn't max out his credit cards. Then there were all those dates with Jenny. She was a prize, and he didn't want her to get away. So with the help of his credit cards, he went out of his way to woo her.

When Bob and Jenny got married, their debts and spending habits came along as part of the package. Instead of solving their financial woes, they had suddenly doubled them. It wasn't long before they couldn't keep up with all the payments. Although they had dreams for the future, like starting a family and buying a house, they couldn't afford to do either. That's when things started to fall apart.

She blamed him for not applying himself. "What's wrong with him? He should have a promotion by now," she thought.

He blamed her for spending too much. "Why does she need all those clothes?"

When the bill collectors started calling, their stress level hit code red. Every time they heard the phone ring, their stomachs churned out of fear that it was another collection call. Going to the mail box was torture; all that seemed to be there were bills, nasty letters from collection agencies, and as if it were a cruel joke, offers for more credit cards.

On bill paying days, the tension was unbearable. They gave each other wide berths on those days and said as little as possible. Neither one wanted to get their head bit off by the other. The honeymoon was definitely over, but ironically it hadn't been paid off yet. They no longer saw each other as the love of their life. Instead they looked at each other as the reason for their ruin. They thought about getting a divorce, but they couldn't even afford that. Their cravings were destroying them.

They can destroy us as well.

The Craving for More

We can't say that we weren't warned. Do you remember these words of wisdom from the last chapter? "Do not love this world nor the things it offers you, for when you love the world, you do not have the love of the Father in you. For the world offers only a craving... for everything we see.... (This is) not from the Father, but... from this world. And this world is fading away, along with everything that people crave. But anyone who does what pleases God will live forever" (1 John 2:15-17).

The "craving for everything we see" is insatiable. No matter how much we have, it seems we are never content. We always want more. In 2003, the Gallup organization did a poll to see how much annual income people felt they would need in order to be rich. The results were fascinating. People who made $30,000 a

> *Those who love money will never have enough. How meaningless to think that wealth brings true happiness! Ecclesiastes 5:10*

year said they would feel rich if they made $75,000. People who made $50,000 a year said they would need to make $100,000. But when they asked people who made $100,000 a year, they said they would need to make $200,000.

Then they asked millionaires how much money they would need to feel rich. They said they would need a portfolio worth at least $5 million dollars. Of course, that was in 2003. According to a 2011 Gallup poll, millionaires now say they need at least $7.5 million dollars to feel rich. If you don't feel rich with a "measly" million dollars, I'm thinking I'd like a shot at being that "poor".

It seems that no matter how much money we have, it's never enough. Being rich is a moving target. This goes to prove the ancient wisdom of the Bible that says, "Those who love money will never have enough. How meaningless to think that wealth brings true happiness!" (Ecclesiastes 5:10)

This craving for everything we see is a huge character issue. You have seen the problems these cravings caused Bob and Jenny, but that's just the tip of the iceberg. Our continual lust for more can do far worse damage.

Losing Our Integrity One Bite at a Time

A person of great character is a person of integrity. Because they can be trusted, they are able to accomplish things that make the world better. However, integrity can be seriously corrupted by our cravings. There's no denying this fact. There is a long, shameful list of corporations and executives who have trampled honesty, compassion, and even the law in a relentless and reckless effort to gain more. Remember Worldcom, Enron, Arthur Anderson, Lehman Brothers, or Bernie Madoff? Thousands of individuals and even entire communities were harmed by their dishonest quest for more.

You may think that these extreme examples have little relevance to your life. Think again. At the root of large scale corruption is the same craving for more that you and I are tempted with. The only difference is that these corporations had greater resources so they were able to cause exponentially greater damage.

When we act on our cravings, our integrity is put in jeopardy as we start spending beyond our means. The temptations might start small. "How much harm can cheating on my taxes cause? I need the money and the government would just waste it." Or you might be tempted to pick up a few extra bucks by cheating on your business expense reports because, "Everyone does it and if everyone does it, it's not really wrong."

Once we compromise on small things, it's easier to compromise on big things. It's just like when I eat cake. I don't want a whole piece because I'm on a diet, but a little nibble won't hurt. But that nibble is so delicious I can't help but have another nibble...and then another...and another. By the time I'm done, I've eaten a whole piece of cake and then some. In much the same way, our integrity is eaten away one small compromise at a time.

When the financial pressure caused by our cravings gets too great, we feel pressured to make bigger compromises. We see a quick fix to our problems by "borrowing" from our work. We tell ourselves we'll be able to replace the money before anyone notices it's missing. Or, we steal from our customers. We don't hold a gun to their head, but we make promises we can't keep in order to make a sale.

Finally, your boss asks you to do something unethical. Be honest. If you're in a deep financial hole, would you risk losing a promotion or even your job by telling your boss "no"?

One bite at a time, our craving for more destroys our integrity and character.

The Insecurity of Cravings

There is also a strong link between our cravings and insecurity. When you feel insecure, you buy more stuff, or you hoard what you have because you believe you'll feel secure once you have enough. Ironically, though, the more you have, the more you have to lose, and that makes you feel insecure. It's like a dog chasing its tail. You'll never win, but you won't stop trying.

As they spin from insecurity, to mistrust, to selfishness, their craving for everything they see destroys their character.

This vicious cycle of insecurity leads to mistrust. When you feel insecure you see others as threats, as people who want to take something from you, or are preventing you from getting what you want. Bob and Jenny are examples of this. They went from holding hands to pointing fingers as their debts increased.

When people feel insecure, they will also cling tighter to their possessions, because they are convinced that they can't afford to lose anything. If they gave anything away it would mean they would have less, and the thought of having less only adds to their feelings of insecurity. Once you mistrust others and refuse to give, you will be incapable of making even a small part of the world around you better—you'll be insignificant.

As I have said before, I believe people are failures when they squander opportunities to make the world better. They may have mountains of stuff, but they have no significance. Their "bling" may make them look good on the outside, but inside they have no substance. Turn-by-turn, as they spin from insecurity, to mistrust, to selfishness, their craving for everything they see destroys their character.

You need to decide if you want to be a person of strong character, who can be counted on and who makes the world better, or if you want to be a person who is known for your cravings, who is insecure, mistrusting and tightfisted, and who makes little difference in other people's lives. What type of person you'll become hinges on a very important decision. It is the decision about whether or not to be generous.

Showing Signs of Maturity

Being a generous giver is the counter-intuitive solution to our destructive cravings for everything we see. Acts 20:35 states, "It is more blessed to give than to receive." It takes maturity to begin to appreciate the wisdom of that verse.

When I was a child, Christmas was the longest night of the year. On any other night I'd put my head on my pillow, snuggle down into my blankets, and the next thing I knew it would be morning. But not on Christmas Eve. On that night, I knew just outside my door was a treasure trove of gifts waiting to be ripped open with gleeful abandon. On that night, I'd toss and turn with anticipation and excitement. On that night, the clock ticked slower—I swear to it. On that night, I thought that whoever said, "It's better to give than to receive," was crazy. (It wasn't until later that I found out it was Jesus who said it—oops.)

I loved to receive gifts as a child, but giving gifts, especially ones I had to buy with my own money, didn't thrill me. As an adult, however, things are different. Now, I enjoy watching my grandkids open up the gifts I've given them. Seeing the delight on their faces, and hearing their shouts of "Yes, yes, yes!" feels—dare I say it—even better than receiving gifts. Do you know what I mean?

It's a sign that you have matured when you enjoy giving more than receiving. The selfish joy of childhood, which is measured by what everyone is doing to make you happy, is replaced by the selfless joy of adulthood, which is measured by how much you are able to do to make others happy. But selfless joy is just one of the many benefits of being generous.

Generosity and Mental Health

Did you know that generosity can protect you from mental illness? It's true. Dr. Karl Menninger was a famous psychiatrist of a generation ago. People would come from around the world to seek his help for their mental disorders. As Dr. Menninger worked with patients, he began to notice that most, if not all, of his patients were selfish. As he studied this phenomenon, he realized that generous people were rarely mentally ill. The reason, Dr. Menninger concluded, was remarkably simple. When you are generous, you are more focused on helping others and less focused on your own problems. Generosity, it seems, creates a simple shift in focus that pays amazing dividends in keeping us emotionally and mentally healthy.

From Victim to Hero

Generosity also leads to feelings of worth and security. When people are insecure they often define their identity by what they have. If they have a lot of stuff, they see themselves as powerful and important, but if they only have a little stuff, they feel deficient and poor. When our identity is tied to stuff, we will always be insecure, because if we were to lose our stuff, we would lose our sense of worth.

Generosity, however, will turn the tables on this self-destructive thinking. The act of generosity breaks the stranglehold your stuff has on your identity. By being generous,

When you focus on what you have, instead of on what you don't have, you'll stop playing the role of a victim and start acting like a hero.

you make a powerful statement that says, "I am more than just the accumulation of my wealth, and I'm willing to prove it by giving it away."

Some people say to me, "I'd like to be generous, but I don't have enough to be generous with." That kind of thinking will only fuel feelings of deficiency. You always have something you can offer that will bless others. It may not be as much as the person next to you, but that's no excuse for being stingy. When you focus on what you have, instead of on what you don't have, you'll stop playing the role of a victim and start acting like a hero.

Soul'd Out

Not long ago, my beautiful wife Charlene said, "I've been wanting some chips all night, and there's none in the house. Would you run down to the gas station and get me some?" It was 11:00 at night.

My initial reaction went something like this: "What's up with you girl? You're not pregnant are you?" After we had a good laugh over that thought, I went out and got my wife some chips. Why? Because I love and treasure her.

My mother used to say over and over again, "You can give without loving, but you can't love without giving." Generosity is a sign of a heart that is soul'd out to God. That is why Jesus said your heart will be where your treasure is (Matthew 6:21). If you love God, you'll invest your treasure with God by being generous.

In God We Trust

Generosity is an act of faith. If we trust in money more than we trust in God, we will struggle to be generous. And it's not hard to understand why we would trust in money more than God. After all, it's money that pays the bills, provides for our needs and allows us to purchase our wants, right?

Not according to Deuteronomy 8:18, which says, "But remember the LORD your God, for it is He who gives you the ability to produce wealth" (NIV). God is the One who created us with the knowledge and ability to earn money.

However, we can get so focused on money that we lose sight of God—who provides the means to earn the money. That is why generosity is so important to God. When we give away our money, we change our focus. We break free of our trust in money and put our trust in God.

Our trust in God also breaks our craving for everything we see. Because we trust God, we no longer feel the need to fill our lives with stuff in a vain effort to feel important or secure. Our security now comes from our relationship to God. We are no longer controlled by our insecurity, and that allows us to give freely.

Make the Most of the Opportunity

Our treasure is a God-given opportunity. 2 Corinthians 9:11 says, "You will be enriched in every way so that you can always be generous. And when we take your gifts to those who need them, they will thank God." God has put resources in our hands that we can use to bless others. He's given us the opportunity to be involved in His work. Now we must prove that we are trustworthy.

Jesus said, "If you are faithful in little things, you will be faithful in large ones. But if you are dishonest in little things, you won't be honest with greater responsibilities. And if you are untrustworthy about worldly wealth, who will trust you with the true riches of heaven?" (Luke 16:10-11).

God has given us the opportunity to bless others and be difference-makers. We need to prove our trustworthiness to God by being generous and making the most of the opportunity. When we show that we are trustworthy, God will trust us with greater resources for accomplishing greater things.

More than just Money

Generosity extends beyond money to also include our time and talent. When we love, when we are soul'd out to God, we give of ourselves, not just of our money. My friend John has been an inspirational example of this for me.

After thirty years of marriage, John's wife, Evie, fell victim to Alzheimer's disease. For many, the onset of Alzheimer's happens gradually, but for Evie it happened all at once. It seemed like one day she was fine, and the next day she wasn't. It wasn't long before Evie didn't even recognize John as her husband. But John still loved Evie.

With few exceptions, John took Evie with him wherever he went. John would even take Evie out to dinner, even though he would have to feed her himself. Every Sunday, John would bring her to our church and reintroduce her to all of her old friends. He would bring Evie up to me and say, "Evie, this is Sherwood. Shake hands and say hi to Sherwood."

One day I invited John to come to a Bible study I was teaching, because I wanted to encourage and strengthen him. John said, "Hey, I'll do anything for you. It's a done deal. I'd love to be there." Then, he looked at his calendar and said, "Wait a minute, I can't do it. I am going to be out on Tuesday and I've already agreed to meet with Evie's folks on Thursday. That means I would be out three nights in a row, and I can't do that. I need to be with her."

I was amazed. Evie didn't even recognize him, but he still wanted to be at home with her. I'm not even sure she would know that John was in the room with her, but still he said to me, "I want to spend time with my wife. She has got to have my time."

John was willing to give his time to somebody who could not give it back, who did not even know who he was. When I saw that, it messed me up. I said, "God I need to change, because that's not me. I need help in being that generous with my time."

John's example of lavish love has been a blessing to all those who have had the honor of witnessing it. John helped me see what loving generosity looked like, and his example has made a huge difference in my own life and in the lives of countless others.

How to be Generous

I'm tempted to say that generosity is "giving until it hurts." However, it's been my observation that it starts to hurt as soon as we pull out our wallet. So let me define generosity differently. Generosity is liberal giving. It is unselfish giving that is above and beyond the call of duty.

My friend John has been a wonderful example of this kind of generosity. So how can we become generous?

Realize you have Something to Give

Some people have the attitude of "I'll be generous when...." "I'll be generous when... I make more money." "I'll be generous when... I have more time." They'll tell me, "I want to be generous, but I have nothing to offer." My response is, "Stop complaining about what you don't have. Stop making excuses. God isn't looking at what you don't have. He wants you to give from what He's given you."

Generosity is not a matter of being rich or poor. It is not about the amount you give. Generosity is about the proportion you give. For example, a $10,000 gift may not be very generous if it comes from someone who makes $200,000 a year, but a $100 gift would be lavish if it came from someone who only makes $1,000.

We all have something to give. God's word tells us in 2 Corinthians 9:10 that "God is the one who provides seed for the farmer and then bread to eat. In the same way, He will provide and increase your resources and then produce a great harvest of generosity in you." So if God has blessed you with a little, give a little. If God has blessed you with a lot, give a lot. And be a blessing to others.

The same is true of being generous with your time and talent. You may have a little or a lot, but the amount doesn't matter. You still have time and talent to offer. It's just a matter of deciding to be generous with whatever you have.

Be Intentional

Generosity doesn't happen by accident. 2 Corinthians 9:7 tells us, "You must each decide in your heart how much to give. And don't give reluctantly or in response to pressure." Generosity is a free choice. It is something we must intentionally *decide* to do.

If you can be an intentional shopper, you can be an intentional giver. Most of us are intentional shoppers. We see something we want, and we start to make a plan on how we can get it. We think, "If I cut back here, if I do a side job there... wow, I'll be able to buy that object of my dreams." Our intentional shopping stretches our resources to the limit and leaves us with nothing to give. We need to reverse that trend.

If we want to be generous, we need to be as intentional about our giving as we are about our spending. Here's an

> *Intentional givers will make a plan for giving more as God provides more.*

example: "If I keep the car a couple more years; if I don't buy that new pair of shoes; if I can be content with the TV I already have, if I cut out one double latte a week, if I downsize instead of upgrade... wow, look at how much I can give!"

Intentional givers will go even farther by making a plan for giving more as God provides more. Most people have a list in mind of all the things they would like to get if they had the money. I have a list like this, and you probably do as well. It might be a special vacation, new furniture, or remodeling the house. Your list is a plan of how you will spend your money if you ever have more. In the same way, we can create a plan for how we will give if we ever have more resources. You can call it your generosity list and it can include all of the ministries and charities you want to give to if God blesses you with more.

Give Now

Don't be a leftover giver. In 2 Chronicles 31:5 we are told that "the people of Israel responded *immediately* and generously by bringing the *first* of their crops and grain, new wine, olive oil, honey, and all the produce of their fields" (*emphasis mine*). The Israelites didn't wait until the harvest was completed to see if they could afford to give. That's not being generous. Instead, the Israelites gave the first of their harvest.

Satan will try to sabotage the blessings we can experience from being generous. He'll whisper in our ear, "Give after you have enough; after you've gotten all you want; after you feel secure." If we listen to that line of thinking, God will get moved to the back of the line and be given the leftovers, assuming there's anything left over. If that is how we dare to treat God, we do not understand who God is.

In contrast, generous people give now of their time, treasure and talent. By giving now, God comes first. So let the first "bill" you pay be your donation to your church and other favorite charities. Before turning on the TV, first spend time catching up with your kids and spouse. And be generous with your talents by serving others one Saturday a month, or every other month. Don't put it off. Decide to be generous now.

Be Cheerful

"Don't give reluctantly or in response to pressure. 'For God loves a person who gives cheerfully'" (2 Corinthians 9:7). When you decide to be generous, something amazing begins to happen. You begin to see God work through your giving to make a difference in someone else's life. When you see the difference you're making, it excites you so much you want to give more. You become a cheerful giver. Now instead of being trapped in a destructive cycle of craving that leads to mistrust and insecurity, your generosity pulls you into a character building cycle of difference-making, that leads to excitement, that leads to joy.

That's when life gets exciting. That's when we reach a point where we truly feel full. Our generosity fills us with joy, and also with a sense of meaning and purpose. Now we understand from our own experience that it is "more blessed to give than to receive."

God Gave...

John 3:16 states, "For God so loved the world that He *gave* His only Son" (*emphasis mine*). Generosity is part of the character of God. It is God's generosity that has made the world better, and our selfishness that has made it worse. Because God gave His only Son, Jesus, we get a second chance at having a relationship with God and becoming someone who is significant.

Generosity is powerful. God has set you an example to follow and given you the means to be generous. Now, the decision is up to you.

Will you break the destructive force of your cravings by choosing to be generous, or you will be sucked into the destructive downward cycle of cravings? The strength of your character, the type of person you will be, the difference you will make, in your family, and in the world, will be determined by your choice.

Decide to Serve

*"We are prone to judge success by the index of our salaries or the
size of our automobiles, rather than by the quality of our service."*
– Martin Luther King, Jr.

John Edwards sat comfortably in his home talking to an interviewer
for the ABC news show *Nightline*. Wearing khakis and a blue pinpoint
shirt, he looked carefree. As he talked, he flashed his trademark smile,
which seemed out of place considering the bombshell admission he just
made.

In 2008, John Edwards was campaigning to be the Democratic candidate for President of the United States. With boyish good looks and
national popularity, he was a natural target for the tabloids. Sure
enough, the *National Enquirer* published a headline-grabbing story that
claimed Edwards was having an affair with a campaign worker. The
story was all the more scandalous because John Edwards' wife of

thirty-plus years had been fighting a very public battle with breast cancer.

Edwards vehemently denied the accusation. Given his popularity and the fact that the accusation came from the *National Enquirer*, a very dubious source, most people gave him the benefit of the doubt. The *Enquirer*, however, didn't back off its story. Instead, it printed more articles with additional tantalizing bits of information.

Finally, after losing his bid to become a presidential candidate, John Edwards invited the *Nightline* news crew to his home for an exclusive interview. The first question asked was, "Did you have an affair?" That's when John Edwards dropped his bombshell. He admitted to the affair he had denied for months.

The interviewer then asked the question that was on everyone's minds: "How could you do this?"

Edwards explained himself by saying, "I grew up as a small town boy in North Carolina. I came from nothing, worked very hard, and hoped that I'd be able to do something helpful for other people. I became a lawyer. Through a lot of work and success, I got some acclaim as a lawyer. People were telling me, 'Oh he's such a great person, such a great lawyer, such a talent. You're going to go (far). (There's) no telling what you'll do.' This was when I was 30, 31 years old. Then, I went to being a senator—a young senator—then being considered for vice-president, running for president, being a vice-presidential candidate and becoming a national public figure. All of which (created) a self-focus, an egotism, a narcissism that leads you to believe that you can do whatever you want; you're invincible and there'll be no consequences."

"So you thought you'd never get caught?" asked the interviewer.

"It was a huge mistake in judgment," Edward's admitted, "but yeah, I didn't think I'd ever get caught."

A Pride that Destroys

The Bible says, "Do not love this world nor the things it offers you, for when you love the world, you do not have the love of the Father in you. For the world offers only a craving for physical pleasure, a craving for everything we see, and *pride in our achievements* and possessions. These are not from the Father, but are from this world. And this world is fading away,

> *Pride erodes the foundations of our character until our life caves in under the weight of our arrogance.*

along with everything that people crave. But anyone who does what pleases God will live forever" (1 John 2:15-17 *emphasis mine*).

John Edwards provides a textbook example of how "pride in our achievements" can erode the foundations of our character, until we reach a point where our life caves in under the weight of our arrogance. Edwards thought so highly of himself that he believed he was "invincible."

John Edwards doesn't stand alone when it comes to pride. There is a long and infamous list of politicians, sports figures, movie stars, business executives and even preachers who have allowed pride in "achievements and possessions" to lead them to self-destruction.

At times, these proud people make the world better, but often the harm they cause outweighs the good they've done. Their self-destruction sends out shockwaves that unfairly damage the lives of countless others. Families, careers, even business empires have been destroyed by the pride of a few—and that's nothing to be proud of.

Not all pride is harmful. I want to make that clear. We can and should feel good about our accomplishments. We should see ourselves as people with spectacular value. After all, we are created in God's image, and God deems us worth dying for. It is a healthy thing to feel pride about our accomplishments and worth.

However, there is another kind of pride that goes beyond feeling good about ourselves, and instead we become "full of ourselves." This is a pride that doesn't just say, "I did well," it says, "I'm better than you." This is a pride that seeks attention, obsesses with status and self-importance, believes it is privileged, expects special treatment, and says, "I can do whatever I want, I'm invincible." This kind of pride will destroy you. Proverbs 16:18 says, "Pride goes before destruction, and haughtiness before a fall."

You are Not Immune

You may think you're immune to this kind of arrogant pride. You may believe that only the famous are susceptible to this type of temptation.

Don't fool yourself. We're all susceptible. 1 Corinthians 10:12 says, "If you think you are standing strong, be careful not to fall."

For example, have you ever felt under-appreciated at work? You think to yourself, "I put in all this effort and someone else gets the accolades while I fetch the coffee. I want some praise. I want someone to fetch me coffee."

Have you ever come home and wanted your family to serve you for a change? "After all, I am the king (or queen) of the castle."

How many couples do you know whose marriages have fallen apart because one or both spouses felt like the other spouse wasn't sufficiently serving their needs? "If she loved me, she would...." To which she responds, "If he loved me, he would...."

This self-destructive, arrogant pride is as seductive as it is corrosive. It is easy to fall under its spell and not wake up until the damage is done.

We've been Warned!

Time and time again the Bible warns us about pride. Here are just a few examples:

> "Therefore, the proud may not stand in your presence, for
> you hate all who do evil" (Psalm 5:5).

> "The Lord detests the proud;
> they will surely be punished" (Proverbs 16:5).

"I, the Lord, will...crush the arrogance of the proud and
humble the pride of the mighty" (Isaiah 13:11).

There can be no doubt how God feels about our pride. Pride not
only destroys our character and our lives, it also destroys our relationship with God.

A Culture of Pride

The reason we are so susceptible to pride is that it permeates our
culture. Pride is like the air we breathe. Our society is based on power,
status, and importance. When you have power you have control.
You're at the top of the food chain and get to call the shots. You can
make stuff happen. When you have status, you sit in the seat others
want to sit in. And when you are important, you get perks. People
strive to be important so they can get in on the perks.

It's amazing to me that we live in a society where, because of our
status, power, or importance, other people will actually serve us.
What's more amazing is that people with status actually expect others
to serve them. This shocks me because people with power, status, and
influence are in a position to make a difference in the world. But
instead of using their tremendous resources to serve others, they expect
to be served.

As a matter of fact, if you look in the Bible, it says, "When someone has been given much, much will be required in return; and when

someone has been entrusted with much, even more will be required" (Luke 12:48). Why don't we have a mentality where we think that, because of our elevated status, we should serve others and make sure they get perks? The answer is: our pride gets in the way.

The Way to Defeat Pride

I am convinced that the God-given antidote to our self-destructive pride is to serve others. Serving and lifting others up is a common theme in the Bible. While the world bases its mantra on power, status, and importance, the Bible calls us to live a life of humility, self-sacrifice and service where we treat others as more important than ourselves.

Jesus said, "You know that the rulers in this world lord it over their people, and officials flaunt their authority over those under them. But among you it will be different. Whoever wants to be a leader among you must be your servant, and whoever wants to be first among you must become your slave. For even the Son of Man came not to be served but to serve others and to give his life as a ransom for many" (Matthew 22:25-28).

The Bible frequently refers to believers as "servants of Christ." Now, "servant" is just a polite way of saying "slave." A person soul'd-out to Christ is really a slave to Christ. Listen to how Paul introduces himself to the believers in Rome: "This letter is from Paul, a slave of Christ Jesus" (Romans 1:1).

To an African-American like myself, the word "slave" dredges up dark memories of brutal abuse and subjugation, when we were thought of and treated as sub-human. Even today, telling African-Americans that they are to be slaves of Christ will receive a chilly response. When I preach on this in my church, I have to say, "Amen, all by myself," because there's not many in the congregation who are getting fired-up by what I'm saying. However, Jesus didn't make a mistake when he told us that, if we want to be first, we must become slaves. Neither did Paul mess up when he called himself a slave of Christ.

> *God our Master...does not take a whip to our backs. Instead, our Master frees us to become fully human.*

A slave is someone who belongs to the master and carries out everything the master asks him to do. As followers of Christ, God is our Master. Did you hear what I said? God is our Master because He is the omnipotent, omnipresent, King of Kings, Lord of Lords, Ruler of Heaven and Earth. But God chose not to use His power and position to force us to be slaves. Instead, God made His claim as our Master by purchasing us from our slavery to sin and the devil—paying for us with His life.

The difference between the slavery of American history and slavery to Christ is as big as the difference between heaven and hell. God our Master is not cruel or oppressive. He does not take a whip to our backs or strip us of our dignity. Instead, our Master frees us to become fully human—to become who He created us to be. So we serve Him as our Master, and through our obedience, we end up experiencing fulfillment.

Unlike human slave owners, our Master loves us and serves us. This is truly mind-blowing. Not only do we serve God, but the Almighty God serves us! And in response to God's love, we go on to serve others as soul'd-out followers of Christ.

When you truly see yourself as a slave, it's nearly impossible to be prideful. Humble service is the antidote to pride. And as we serve, God's power works within us to defeat pride and strengthen our character.

It Ain't Sexy

Serving, however, is not sexy. It's not appealing to most folks. Let's be honest, most of us would rather *be* served than *to* serve. It's easier to sit back and have everything come to us than it is to get up and say, "You know what? I am going to serve other people."

I'll be honest with you, I struggle with serving. I try to serve my family, but there are times when I feel like they should be doing more to meet my needs. And I work hard to serve my congregation, but there are times I wish they'd do more to serve me. I'm not proud of feeling this way, but I want to keep it real with you. There are times I forget that I am a slave of Christ, and in those moments pride pounces and starts messing with my mind.

Flipping the Script

Sometimes, however, we flip the script. Instead of saying, "I'm too important to serve," we say, "I'm not important enough to serve." This became clear to me when I went along on a mission trip to Mexico with a large group of teenagers from the suburbs. The teens were all from Bayside Church of Granite Bay, California.

Granite Bay is an affluent suburb nestled against Folsom Lake, just outside of Sacramento. But this suburban church had a vision to plant a new church in the city. I was the guy they recruited to launch this new church, and to help me prepare they brought me onto their church staff. Next thing I know, I'm being sent along with their youth group on a mission trip to Mexico.

The trip was eye-opening for me. I was with hundreds of well-to-do teenagers. They were the kind of kids who, because of their affluence, you'd expect to be stuck up and act superior towards others. But it was just the opposite. These kids relished serving.

While in Mexico, they worked eight to ten hours a day. They lived in a compound that was nothing more than a dirt field. They slept in tents on rickety camp cots or the ground. When a breeze blew, clouds of dust would fly through camp. There were no bathrooms, just pit toilets. They got one shower all week, and to get it, they had to go into town and pay for it. It was a far cry from life at home, but these teenagers ate it up. Hot, dirty, sweaty, smelly, tired, and sore they threw themselves into working day after day for an entire week, and had the time of their lives.

I'm not proud of this, but as an urban guy I had some opinions about suburban kids. I expected them to be soft. I expected them to have attitude. I didn't expect them to be so eager to serve. But as I watched, I thought, "My God, these kids from the suburbs are teaching me what it means to serve."

I decided immediately that the church I was starting would duplicate this experience because in urban culture, unfortunately, there is this unconscious feeling that we are too deprived to serve. Since there are people around us in the suburbs who are doing better than us, we feel we have nothing to offer. Instead, we think that we're the ones needing to *be* served.

The reality is that everyone has something to offer, even supposedly "deprived" folks. Amen, all by myself! It is when we serve that we realize we have something to offer, and our self-defeating, "poor little ole me" feelings go away. Through helping others, we start to believe in our capabilities, we start making a difference, and our character gets strengthened. I'm excited to say that our urban church now sends our teens on a mission trip every year, so that at an early age they can develop the character trait of serving, and they begin to realize that they can be difference-makers.

Some people feel too important to serve, others feel too unimportant. Either way, the result is the same. Your character is weakened when you fail to serve.

Inconvenient

Another excuse we use to keep from serving is that it's inconvenient. In Mexico, our contact person was a former beauty queen who now served the poor of her community. She knew where all the needs were in her community, and arranged for all of our service projects. She told us about a village that desperately needed a food storage locker built along with a home for the family who would oversee the food locker. She explained that this project would be an unbelievable blessing to this impoverished village.

"Could you do it?" She tentatively asked.

"Sure," we said, "we'd be glad to do that."

Then came the catch—the village was nearly a four hour round trip from our base camp. We started backpedaling and making excuses.

People across this country are not serving because it's inconvenient. That's not being soul'd out!

"Ahhh, we don't think we can do that. It's too far. We'd be too separated. It would be unsafe. What if something went wrong between here and there? Can't you find needy people a little closer to here? You know, so it's convenient for us."

Well, it didn't take long before we were convicted of our non-servant attitude. We took on the project, and today that village is blessed with the food locker they desperately needed, along with a new home for its manager.

It baffles me why we expect serving to be convenient. Where did we get the idea? Service is not convenient.

I guarantee you it was not convenient for Jesus to leave heaven and come to earth. I guarantee it was not convenient for Him to spend nine months in a womb. I guarantee it was not convenient for Him to go to the cross. When Jesus served, He sacrificed something, He gave up something. Service is sacrifice.

There are people across this country—Christians—who are not serving because it's inconvenient. Serving just doesn't fit their schedule. What?!! That's not the way of Christ. That's not being soul'd out! If there's no sacrifice, if nothing is being given up, then it's not service!

In 2 Corinthians 4:5 Paul says, "We ourselves are your servants for Jesus' sake." Did you get that? We don't serve for our own convenience. We serve for the sake of Jesus. We are slaves for Christ and a slave doesn't serve only when it suits him. Amen, all by myself!

Attitude Check

The battery had died in one of the smoke detectors at my house and it began to beep. You know how annoying that beeping is, right? Of course, it had to be one o'clock in the morning when the beeping started. I swear that there's an unwritten rule that says smoke detector batteries can only die in the middle of the night.

My wife said to me, "Hey, could you fix that? I can't go to sleep with that noise."

We didn't have any 9-volt batteries in the house, so I did the next best thing. I took the battery out of the smoke detector. "There," I thought, "that should fix the problem until I get around to getting a new battery." I climbed back in bed, pulled the covers up and…beep. The detector went off again.

What I didn't know was that the smoke detectors were all wired to my home's electrical system. The battery was only an emergency backup in case the power went out. As far as the smoke detector was concerned, a missing battery wasn't any different than a dead battery, so it continued with its beeping.

My wife rolled over and looked at me with that what-are-you-going-to-do-about-it look. Because I am a good husband, and I love my wife dearly, I did what all good husbands do. I got back out of bed, walked to our bedroom door, closed it, and came back to bed. I then dared to tell Charlene, "With the door closed, it shouldn't be loud enough to keep us awake."

My wife felt differently.

"If you really concentrate I'm sure you'll be able to go to sleep," I said. "In fact, I'll rub your back to help you fall asleep."

That did not win her over. "I cannot believe you're not going to fix that!" she said.

"Honey, I can't. We don't have a battery."

"I cannot fall asleep with that smoke detector beeping."

"What do you want me to do? I am in my pajamas. It's one o'clock in the morning. Do you expect me to get up, go to a convenience store, and buy a battery?" Here's a lesson I learned that night: you shouldn't ask questions you don't want answers to.

"Yes," my wife said.

I'd like to tell you that I had a really good attitude through all of this, but I didn't. It was one o'clock in the morning, and this was inconvenient. I got out of bed, threw on some sweats, went out, bought a ridiculously overpriced battery from a mini-mart, came home, and fixed the smoke detector.

Charlene was then able to quickly fall asleep, but I laid there wide awake. I was being convicted. I heard the Spirit of the Lord asking me, "How are you going to serve other people if you won't even serve your wife?" It was an attitude check.

Serving isn't convenient. Serving is not about you. Serving is about meeting the needs of others, whether it's convenient or not.

You Must Decide to Serve

Often we treat serving as an add-on, something we do occasionally (usually when it's convenient). We don't treat it as a character trait that defines us. But serving is one of Jesus' defining characteristics. As followers of Christ, serving needs to become one of our defining characteristics as well.

However, this is easier said than done. Serving does not come naturally. Most of us don't wake up in the morning thinking, "Who can I serve today?" We live in a selfish world, and we have developed habits and cravings that will not disappear easily.

Because serving does not come naturally, we need to make serving an *intentional decision*. We need to intentionally look for ways to serve others. By choosing to serve, we'll be breaking up old, prideful habits and replacing them with new habits that are in step with God. Then, as we walk in step with God, we gain His strength to defeat our self-destructive pride.

Don't Give Pride an Opportunity

Many people fail simply because they don't stay busy serving God. King David may be the poster boy for this kind of failure. David was a warrior, but he reached a point in his life where he felt that he was too important to go to war. So David sent his troops out with his second-in-command, while he stayed home. Next thing you know, David is a peeping Tom, having an affair, and conspiring to commit murder. His self-destructive pride ended up inflicting incredible pain on the entire nation of Israel.

The temptation to be prideful is always lurking nearby, ready to jump in and wreak havoc in our lives the moment we give it an opportunity. But when I am on the right road, consciously choosing to serve others, I'm too busy doing what God wants me to do to give pride an opportunity to pounce.

Opportunities to Serve

To defeat pride, we need to figure out how we can serve others. I believe the best place to start is with our families. If you want to move your family forward, find out what their needs are, and then with the help of God, begin to meet those needs. Don't focus on how your family can better serve you—that will only make a mess. Instead, find out what your wife needs, or your husband wants. Find out what your son or daughter is longing for. Ask your mom or dad what you can do to help them around the house.

One member in your family may need help with chores. Another member may need to talk and would be thrilled if you asked questions and showed interest in their interests. Another may need a hug. The best thing you could do for your wife may be to take the kids and give her some free time. Maybe your husband would like you to surprise him and take him on a date. Your kids may need help with homework, or just want some play time with you. Playing Barbie may not be your cup of tea, but remember, you're serving them. Your service will make a world of difference by setting an example that will shape the character of your children.

From serving your family, you can move on to looking for ways to serve your friends. What are their needs? How can you bless them? What project are they working on that you could help them finish? What could you take off their plate that would make their life a little easier?

What about your co-workers? You can ask the same questions. Your workplace is filled with opportunities to serve. What a difference your service will make in their lives, and it will also make a difference in how they feel towards you.

There are always opportunities to volunteer at the local school. Ask your kid's teacher if you can help in the classroom, or stop by the school office and offer your time.

Church, I hope, is an obvious place to serve. In fact, God has wired us to serve in the body of Christ. Churches can never have enough volunteers. Check the church bulletin, listen to the announcements, or call the office to volunteer yourself. A pastor friend of mine recently had a man walk into his office and say he had just started coming to the church and had arranged his schedule so that he could volunteer twenty hours a week doing whatever they needed him to do. (Don't worry, after my friend fainted, they were able to revive him with a couple of slaps to the face).

Finding a place to serve is easy...Wanting to serve is the hard part.

Not only can you serve *at* the church, you can also serve *through* the church. Many churches are involved in community and worldwide service and ministry. Next time your church announces a project, volunteer!

Finding places to serve is easy. We are surrounded by opportunities. Wanting to serve is the hard part. That's why you need to be intentional. Look for an opportunity, then step up and serve. As you do, you will be able to defeat pride before it can defeat you.

Caution: Pride is Sneaky

Pride can be sneaky, twisting our service into another opportunity to be boastful. We all like receiving recognition for our efforts, so when we serve, there's always going to be a temptation to want recognition for the great work we are doing. We need to be careful not to call attention to our service. If we gain any recognition from serving, it should come from someone else and not from ourselves. Proverbs 27:2 says, "Let someone else praise you, not your own mouth—a stranger, not your own lips."

The feeling of not being appreciated is a challenge in my own life. There are times when I feel like I should be getting more credit. I feel like I should be getting more pats on the back and "atta-boy" congratulations. Whenever I feel that way, it's a red flag that I'm headed towards pride.

I can always tell when I am not close to God. I get funky desires and crazy thoughts. I want to draw attention to myself and to my wonderful list of accomplishments. I start complaining about being ignored. However, the moment I start feeling underappreciated is the moment I have stopped humbly serving. In that moment, pride takes over and starts to gnaw away at my character.

My need for appreciation, gratitude, and recognition goes away when I am focused on who I'm serving rather than on myself. When I am busy humbly serving, my pride is pushed out of my life.

If others choose to talk about your service, that's okay. And it's okay if they want to brag about you to other people—just don't jump on their bandwagon. But if no one says a word about all your wonderful service, that's still okay. You are not serving for praise and accolades. You are serving because you have made a character decision. You have decided that you must serve other people, or be destroyed by pride.

Who Will You Be?

What kind of person do you want to be? Do you want to be known for your arrogance; known for your demands; known as someone who wants to be noticed, praised and served? Do you want to be known, (as John Edwards will now always be known), for your pride-fueled self-destruction?

Pride in your accomplishments and possessions will erode your character, until you collapse in self-destruction. To protect yourself from this kind of destructive pride, you must intentionally engage in opportunities to serve others. This is a make-it-or-break-it decision that will define who you will be as a person.

Do you want to be known for your arrogance and pride-fueled self-destruction?

At our best, with all of our degrees, with all the letters after our names, with all the honors on the wall that say how great we are, and with all the trophies we have on our shelves, we are still just slaves. And at the end of life's journey, when we stand before God, He is not going to say: "You did really good, preacher," or "You were an amazing physician," or "You were an out of this world teacher." God is not going to say any of that stuff. Instead, God is going to say, "Well done my good and faithful *servant*" (Matthew 25:21, *emphasis mine*). What God cares about is whether or not you've been a good slave. So use your accomplishments and possessions to serve others, and make a difference in their lives. Make the choice to be a slave for Christ.

Decide to be Soul'd Out

*"Until you have given up your self to Him
you will not have a real self."*
–C.S. Lewis

A few years ago I bought a new wireless printer for my computer. I was really excited to finally be free from cords and be able to work from anywhere in the house. As soon as I got the printer home, I took it out of the box, plugged it in, went to my laptop and eagerly clicked "print". Nothing happened. I tried again—still nothing. I was freaking out. I had a brand new printer that was supposed to make my life better, but it wasn't working.

My son came to my rescue. "Um, papa," he said, "did you load the printer's software on your computer? The printer won't work without the software." I had no idea that before the printer could work I had to load software onto my laptop—probably because I didn't bother to read the instructions. I was a bit embarrassed.

To Run the Program, You need the Software

In this book, we have talked about becoming people of significance—people who make wise choices, people who make the world better. To be that kind of person, you must make some crucial character decisions. You must decide to: be courageous, avoid anger, choose forgiveness, be content, be generous, and serve others. If you make these decisions, it will build a foundation for a great life. But if you decide to not do these things, the results will be disastrous—not only for you, but for your family and friends as well.

It's not enough just to make these decisions...you need to keep them.

I hope I've impressed upon you that these decisions are vital to your well-being. They will help you build a rock-solid life. But it's not enough to just *make* these decisions. There's more to it. Once you make these decisions, you need to *keep* these decisions and make them a permanent part of your life. To do that, you're going to need the "software" to "run the program."

Some people try to use willpower to run their program. Willpower is great. It's an important part of building character. But it's still not enough. In my own life, I have experienced enough failures of willpower to know that willpower is not enough. I am certain the same is true for you.

Having an accountability partner—someone who will help you make and keep these decisions—is another beneficial way to find the strength to "run the program." In fact, I highly recommend that you find a friend and work through this book together.

Accountability is a big step in the right direction, but even that will not be enough. Although accountability can help you combat the destructive cravings that will fight against your character, it won't take the cravings away.

You want to get to a place where these six decisions become a natural and permanent part of your character. That's what this final decision is about. This final decision will "program" you in such a way that the rest of these decisions become the "default program" of your life—a natural part of your character.

Being "Soul'd Out"

So here it is—the final decision. You must decide to be a "soul'd out" follower of Christ. When you make this decision, you gain God's supernatural power to fuel all the other character building decisions.

What do I mean by being "soul'd out"? Let me describe it to you this way. Have you ever watched how people at the beach enter the water? Some people are toe-dippers, others are slow waders, and some are kamikazes.

The toe-dippers will walk to the water's edge, timidly stick their toe in and then stand there trying to decide whether to take another step. I compare the toe-dippers to people who have just said "yes" to Christ or prayed the "Sinner's Prayer."

With that decision, they have received salvation as a free gift of God's grace (Ephesians 2:8-9). All the benefits that come from Jesus' death and resurrection are now theirs. By faith they now have forgiveness, God's presence, the power of the Holy Spirit, and eternal life. At this point, they have stuck their toe in the waters of faith and become pursuers of Christ. Everything is new, and they have a lot to learn. Believers at this early stage of faith may think they're soul'd out, but few really are.

Next are the waders. They slowly walk into the water step-by-tortuous-step, trying to get used to the temperature before diving in all the way. The waders can be compared to believers who have made the decision to start growing in Christ and are now adjusting to the changes that are required.

You need to understand, spiritual growth doesn't happen by accident. The Bible says, "...train yourself to be godly. 'Physical training is good, but training for godliness is much better, promising benefits in this life and in the life to come'" (1 Timothy 4:7-8). Spiritual growth is the result of "training". You need to decide to take intentional steps in order to grow and experience the blessings of your salvation.

Believers at this stage have moved on from dipping their toes in the water. They are now ready to learn how to grow, and they are ready to start taking steps of obedience. But because they are spiritual toddlers, their first steps will be tentative. As they soak in the Bible's teachings, their attitudes and lifestyles are going to be challenged. There will likely be times when they think to themselves, "Jesus wants me to do what? That's crazy!"

Spiritual growth at this stage is often hit or miss, as believers pick and choose what parts of the Bible they're willing to follow and what parts they will conveniently ignore. However, whenever they decide to take a step of obedience, they find that God is right there giving them the strength to succeed. As they get "used to the temperature" of God working in their lives, they're ready to go deeper.

Finally, there are the beach kamikazes. You know who these people are—they're the ones who go barreling into the water and dive-in head first. That's a picture of being soul'd out to Christ. There's no holding back. They have decided to totally surrender to Christ. They are going to completely follow His directions. There's no more testing the water, no more slowly wading in, no more picking and choosing what they will obey and what they will ignore. They have decided to obey Jesus—period. They are soul'd out.

Salvation is Free, but...

I like to say "Salvation is free, but discipleship is going to cost you everything." Although there are great benefits to being soul'd out to Jesus, there is also a great cost. Until you understand and accept the cost, you will never be soul'd out. Otherwise, when you discover the cost, you might decide the price is too high and bail out instead.

In Matthew 16:24, Jesus describes a soul'd out disciple like this: "If any of you wants to be my follower, you must turn from your selfish ways, take up your cross, and follow me."

Take a close look at the progression in this verse. First, you must decide to turn away from something—your selfish ways. Second, you must decide to do something—take up your cross. Only then are you truly following Him. Only then are you truly soul'd out.

There is only one reason you would take up a cross—it's because you're on your way to your own crucifixion.

Jesus is saying, "There are people who think they're following me, but if they're still running their lives and pursuing their desires, they're not really followers. It doesn't matter how much Christian lingo they know, or how much they associate with other believers, or how much they go to church. If they're not killing off their selfish desires, then they're not following me. They are not soul'd out."

If we want to be people who decide to be significant, we've got to turn from our selfish ways. Then, we must take the next step and pick up our cross. That is what being soul'd out is about—taking up our cross. As I see it, there's only one reason you would take up a cross— it's because you're on the way to your own crucifixion.

In our Western culture, we have made Christianity convenient. We have emphasized the free gift of salvation, but not the cost of discipleship. We say, "Hey, pray the 'Sinner's Prayer' and then when the hellfire and brimstone come, you'll be saved." However, I am forced to move past this superficial understanding of following Christ when I realize that being soul'd out means that I'm headed towards my own crucifixion.

Following Christ is not going to be convenient. There is nothing convenient about taking up the cross. Following Christ is going to cost me everything.

When I follow Jesus, I follow Him to my own crucifixion. This is the clear teaching of the Bible. For example, in Galatians 2:20 Paul says, "My old self has been *crucified* with Christ. It is no longer I who live, but Christ lives in me" (*emphasis mine*). So what does it mean to take up my cross, and what will a crucified life look like?

Your Desires are not your Own

When I turn from my selfish ways and take up my cross, it means I cease taking directions from myself. I stop letting my selfish desires and cravings make my choices for me. Instead, as a soul'd out follower of Christ, I nail my wants, dreams, and aspirations to the cross and replace them with God's desires.

Surrendering your desires to God is the price you pay to follow Christ. It is not easy to do. In fact, for me it has been a very difficult price to pay.

I have never fathered my own biological children. My son and daughter are technically my step-children, but because I have always embraced them as my own, I proudly call them my son and daughter. But I have always had a strong desire to father my own biological children as well. God, however, has not allowed me to have that experience. This unfulfilled desire bothered me for years. So I finally decided to talk about it with one of my greatest spiritual mentors—my mom.

My mom was the bomb. She was a strong, African-American woman who loved God with all her heart and raised her family well. She was sensitive to the Spirit of God and seemed to know just the right thing to say in any situation.

I went to her one day near the end of her life and asked, "Mom, have you ever been disappointed, or asked God why I didn't give you any grandchildren?"

She looked at me with a little smile on her face and said, "No, I never asked God that, because you have given me grandchildren. All the children that call you dad are my grandchildren."

My mom was talking about more than just my own stepson and stepdaughter. I have been blessed with the opportunity to influence a number of kids who have no dad in their lives. These kids literally go around town and call me their "dad". As you can imagine, it has created some confusion and embarrassment.

When Charlene and I were married, she had not yet met all these "godchildren" of mine. But after we were married, they started popping up everywhere. People would walk up to my wife and say, "Hey, I met your son." And she'd say, "Oh, you met Anthony." They would get this funny look on their face and say, "No, his name wasn't Anthony."

My wife, understandably, wanted an explanation. We laugh about it now.

I had never thought much about the many children who called me "dad". Thanks to my mom's wisdom, it occurred to me that through my obedience, I had left a legacy in the lives of all these kids. I realized that as long as I was doing God's will I didn't have to chase my own desires. God would take care of everything according to His "good, pleasing and perfect will" (Romans 12:3, NIV). It was God's will that I not father my own children, and I am content with that because God is still using me to leave a legacy.

Now pay attention. I want you to get what I am about to say. My unfulfilled desire to have my own children could have

The decision to be soul'd out to Christ keeps selfish desires from ruining our lives.

created frustration and torn me apart emotionally. My desire could have seduced me into doing something stupid that would have torn apart many lives. But it didn't. That's not to say that I was never tempted, but my decision to be "soul'd out" prevented that temptation, and so many others, from taking root in my life.

People wreck their lives all the time in their efforts to fulfill their selfish desires. By the grace of God this didn't happen to me, because I had made a decision to be soul'd out to Christ. That decision protected me, and it kept selfish desires from overrunning my life. If I had let my unfulfilled desire take over my decision-making, the only legacy I would be leaving would be a legacy of frustration, disappointment, and hurt.

Being soul'd out means you crucify your desires—they are no longer your own. When you are soul'd out, you live for God's desires. That can be a big price to pay. It was hard for me to let go of my desire to father my own children. But God's in charge. I have put my trust in Him. My life is under His control.

This connects well with the wisdom of 1 Peter 4:1-2 which says, "Since Christ suffered physical pain, you must arm yourselves with the same attitude he had, and be ready to suffer, too. For if you have suffered physically for Christ, you have finished with sin. You won't spend the rest of your lives chasing your own desires, but you will be anxious to do the will of God."

An amazing thing happens when you completely surrender your desires to God. You get new desires. You start to desire the things God desires. Psalm 37:4 says, "Take delight in the Lord, and He will give you the desires of your heart" (NIV). This verse isn't saying that your selfish desires will be fulfilled because you follow God. Instead, this verse says that when you are soul'd out, God's desires get transplanted in you. Your heart becomes like His. His desires become your desires.

When you desire what God desires, then your life will be in tune with God's life. God's desires, rather than selfish desires, become your "default program." Your internal life will be at peace and the frustration, disappointment and damage caused by selfish cravings will be crucified.

Your Money is not your Own

Another change that happens when we're soul'd out to God is that we realize our money is not really ours. It belongs to God. Psalm 24:1 says, "The earth is the LORD's, and everything in it. The world and all its people belong to him." But surrendering our money decisions to God is a high price to pay to follow Christ. We want to be in charge of our money and do whatever we please with it. After all, our money is what buys the things we desire.

Growing up, my family was po'. Matter of fact, we were so po', we couldn't even afford the second "o" and the "r" to spell poor. We had

I'm embarrassed to say it, but too often I was serving money...That's not being soul'd out.

most of the necessities, but we didn't have many nice things. So when I began to have some money of my own, I started spending it on all those nice things I was deprived of when I was growing up. As a result, I became a free spirit when it came to spending. This was not good for my finances, my marriage or my soul. My free spending created stress and arguments, but it never offered satisfaction. I always had a craving for more.

Jesus teaches us in Matthew 6:24 that "No one can serve two masters, for you will hate one and love the other; you will be devoted to one and despise the other. You cannot serve both God and money." I'm embarrassed to say it, but too often I was serving money and not God. That's not being soul'd out.

My wife and I are now working to get more financial discipline and structure in our lives. Our desire is to get to a place financially where we will be ready and able to act whenever the Lord says, "I want you to do...." We don't want to be in a place where, because we misused God's money, we would be unable to serve and fulfill God's desires.

God is our Provider—it's His money and we manage it for His glory. It is now time to make the decision to follow Him by saying, "What do you want done with your money? What would please you? This is yours, not mine. This money belongs to you." That's being soul'd out.

Your Destiny is not your Own

I hear people say that you need to make your own destiny. I don't think that's true. If I am soul'd out to God, then my destiny is in His hands. It is God who gets to shape me. I am putty in His hands. God is the One who determines how far I rise and what I become. Isaiah 64:8 says, "We are the clay, and you (God) are the potter. We all are formed by your hand." It's freeing when you know that your destiny is in God's hands.

Bill was a guy who needed to experience this kind of freedom. Bill's boss was retiring and someone in his office was likely to get promoted to fill the vacancy. Bill was a career climber. He dreamed of someday reaching the executive suite. He saw it as his destiny. He dreamed of all he could accomplish, the prestige he would gain, the boost it would give his career, not to mention the increase in his take-home pay.

As he thought about the possibility of getting promoted, Bill's emotions were all over the map. He would get excited, anxious, hopeful, doubtful, and even suspicious of anyone in the office who might also be seeking the promotion.

Bill began schmoozing, manipulating, and scheming. He started looking at his coworkers differently, judging them, trying to determine how his qualifications stacked up against theirs. He discreetly drew attention to himself while he slyly undermined others. He convinced himself that he was the obvious choice for the job.

Bill was crushed when he was told he would not be offered the promotion. His excitement gave way to frustration and depression. His confidence was shaken. What was wrong with him? Why didn't they like him?

When he learned that a coworker, (whom he deemed inferior), was getting the promotion, he became angry and bitter. With his downward spiraling attitude, he was shooting himself in the foot. If his attitude didn't change, there was little chance he would ever be promoted in the future. He'd be lucky just to keep his job. Bill needed to learn this truth: when you try to control your destiny, it ends up controlling you.

Psalm 75:6-7 says, "For promotion comes neither from the east, nor from the west, nor from the south. But God is the judge: He puts down one, and sets up another" (KJV). When you are soul'd out to Christ, you put your destiny where it belongs—in God's hands. You let God control the outcomes of your life. This does not mean you sit around and do nothing. On the contrary, as a representative of Christ you always try to do your best work. You actively look for every opportunity God puts in your path. But you leave the outcomes to God.

Trusting your destiny to God takes away all the manipulation and the funkiness. You can relax.

It is such a peace when you can trust your destiny to God. There will no longer be any more junk about, "I'm not where I'm supposed to be. I didn't get it done. I blew it. I didn't make this happen." There is no longer any driven need to try to force something to happen. There is no longer any self-pity, wondering, "What has my life amounted to?"

Trusting your destiny to God takes away all the mind games, the manipulation, the politics, and the funkiness. Instead of being anxious, you can relax. Instead of being frustrated, you can be joyful. Instead of being judgmental, you can be encouraging. Instead of being angry, you can celebrate. And instead of being bitter, you can forgive.

Because you are soul'd out to Christ, you realize you don't have to be promoted to be successful, you don't have to achieve greatness to be significant, and you don't have to compromise your integrity to be valued.

Your Life is not your Own

Psalms 31:15 says, "My life is in (God's) hands." When you are soul'd out to God, you accept this truth. You no longer fight God for control of your life, nor do you have to worry about what will happen to you.

Jesus said, "I tell you not to worry about everyday life...your heavenly Father already knows all your needs. Seek the Kingdom of God above all else, and live righteously, and he will give you everything you need" (Matthew 6:25, 32-33).

The great thing about that verse is that it's so practical. Because you don't have to worry about your life, you don't have to be controlled by people's opinions of you. You are in God's hands. The only opinion that matters is God's, and we already know what God thinks of you. God thinks you are worth dying for.

When you are in God's hands, you also don't have to be controlled by your fears. God's in control. As a result, you can be courageous. Hebrews 13:6 says, "The LORD is my helper, so I will have no fear. What can mere people do to me?"

When you are in God's hands, you can also boldly serve others because you are unafraid of losing stature. You can be extravagantly generous because you are unafraid of losing possessions. You can be free in forgiveness because you are unafraid of someone taking advantage of you. And you can dare to love others because you are unafraid of being crushed by rejection—you know you're loved by God.

Even the fear of death has no power over you when you are a soul'd out follower of Christ, because you know that you will be resurrected with Christ. This was the hope that kept the Apostle Paul going while he was a prisoner. Even though he knew he might die in prison, he was able to say, "To me, living means living for Christ, and *dying is even better*" (Philippians 1:21, *emphasis mine*).

Death is not a sad, miserable, or depleting thing—it's actually a promotion. I know it's kind of weird to think about death this way. But for people who are soul'd out, that's how they live.

Giving God control of our lives seems like a high price to pay to follow Christ, but I believe the high price is really paid by those who will not surrender to God.

Fill 'er Up

Eternal life is certainly an incredible benefit of being soul'd out to Christ. But that's just the beginning—there's so much more!

When we are soul'd out, our lives get filled with the presence of God. The Bible describes this filling as being "made complete with all the fullness of life and power that comes from God" (Ephesians 3:19). When your life is filled with the fullness of God's life, there is no longer any room for selfish desires and cravings, there is no space for fear, and there is no reason to nurse a grudge. These things get shoved out of our lives by God's expanding presence.

As you are filled with God's life, other things begin to pale in comparison. You wonder how you could ever have been attracted by physical lusts, shiny baubles, or the praise and admiration of mere human beings. Now, your craving is for God. You want to experience as much of God as you can. And when you have a craving for God, you won't crave the things of the world.

God's presence in a soul'd out life will inspire courage, cool down anger, empower forgiveness, bring contentment, motivate generosity and create a desire to serve. In short, God's presence fuels all of the character decisions we've talked about in this book. When we are soul'd out, God fills us with the power we need to maintain the decisions that build rock solid character and lead to a life of significance.

The One and Only Reason to be Soul'd Out

As attractive as all of these benefits are, I don't want you making the decision to be soul'd out based only on "what's in it for me." That is a poor reason for being soul'd out, and it won't hold up during dry times, when you are not "feeling the love."

As followers of Christ, there will be times when God will bring us into the wilderness. Wilderness experiences are the dry times in our lives when the blessings don't seem to flow. Our money is tight, or our health is bad, or the kids are in trouble, or we're unemployed, or we have an enemy determined to make our lives miserable. God allows us to have these experiences to further prepare us to "do the good things He planned for us long ago" (Ephesians 2:10). In my previous book, *Amen All By Myself*, I talk in depth about how God uses these wilderness experiences for our benefit.

If the only reason we are soul'd out is for the blessings we get out of it, we will bail out on God during wilderness times. We need a more compelling reason.

As far as I am concerned, there is only one reason to be soul'd out to Christ—it is because He is GOD! He is Almighty, omnipresent, and all-knowing. He is the King of Kings and Lord of Lords! He is without beginning or end. He is love. He is justice. He is life. He is Creator! Don't let me say, "Amen all by myself!"

If you believe in God but think you can get away with not being soul'd out, you do not understand who God is.

What other response can we have but to surrender ourselves to our Creator God? If we choose not to be soul'd out, we are rejecting God's God-ness!

Poking a grizzly in the nose, pulling a lion's tail, swatting a hornet's nest, or going over the Niagara Falls in a barrel wouldn't be as foolish as choosing to *not* be soul'd out to God. If you believe in God but think you can get away with not being soul'd out to Him, you do not understand who God is.

Don't get me wrong. I'm not suggesting that we follow God out of fear. On the contrary, we follow God out of love and respect. Normally, the thought of submitting to someone else's control is frightening because we do not trust them. We believe that people in control are likely to look out for their own good at the expense of ours. With God, things are different.

God looks out for our good more than He looks out for His own. In fact, "God loved the world so much that he gave his one and only Son, so that everyone who believes in him will not perish but have eternal life" (John 3:16). Our great, awesome, all-powerful God loves us more deeply than we can fathom. So we don't surrender to God unwillingly because we fear His terrifying might. Instead, we respond to His overwhelming love by willingly surrendering to the God we can trust with our lives.

What has a Hold of You?

Jeff had money to burn and he liked to burn it. He enjoyed the best that life could offer—the finest clothes, the biggest homes, and the fanciest means of transportation. Jeff was also shrewd with his money. He used his wealth and status to befriend influential people in high places. He could also be generous. He was a major benefactor to numerous causes and charities.

To say Jeff was "set" in life would be an understatement. But something was bothering Jeff. There was a question that was gnawing at him. He wasn't sure about what would happen to him in the afterlife. You see, Jeff was a religious man. He believed in God and in heaven and hell, and he clearly had a preference for heaven. He wanted to be sure that heaven was where he was headed.

Jeff heard of a new preacher in town who was making waves. This preacher supposedly had a healing ministry that was nothing short of miraculous. And it didn't matter to this preacher what side of the track you were from, he treated everyone as a friend. But being a friend didn't stop this preacher from "getting in your grill." He challenged people to change course, clean up their lives, give up their vices, and serve God. Jeff hoped this preacher would have the answers he was looking for.

When Jeff went to meet the preacher, he figured his status would get him right in. He was shocked, but then impressed, that he had to wait in line with everyone else.

Jeff was pretty good at sizing people up, so when he finally got in to see the preacher, he realized that the usual introductory small talk would be a waste of time. Time with the preacher was precious. Besides, Jeff had the feeling that this preacher had already sized him up and had him figured out. So, Jeff got straight to the point.

"Preacher, what must I do to be sure of eternal life?"

The preacher replied, "Why do you ask me that? You already know the answer. Keep the Ten Commandments."

Jeff was relieved, but not satisfied.

"I've been raised to keep the Ten Commandments. I've been keeping them since my dad taught them to me as a little child. Is that really all there is to it?"

The preacher smiled and then added one more comment. "You're off to a great start. You've laid a great foundation, but there is one more thing. Take what you have and give it away. If you want, sell it and give the money to charity. Then come join me. I want you on my team."

Jeff's face fell. He wasn't ready for that answer. He couldn't even believe what he heard. "Surrender my wealth and fine living? You've got to be kidding," he thought to himself. "My wealth is the source of my security, influence and power. My wealth is my life. I'd be crazy to surrender it."

Jeff walked away sad, with his questions about eternal life still gnawing at him. He never joined the preacher's team.

This encounter occurred between a rich young ruler and Jesus. You can read about it in Mark chapter 10. I admit, I took a few liberties in retelling the story, but I wanted to make a point. I believe we live in a "Rich Young Ruler" society. It wasn't hard to picture Jeff in today's world, was it? People want a convenient faith. They want the free gift of salvation without the cost of following Jesus. But that's not being soul'd out.

Mark 10:22 says that the rich young ruler went away sad because "he had many possessions." But when I preach it, I like to flip the script and say that "his many possessions…had him." And that makes me wonder—what has a hold of you?

All-In

When you are soul'd out, it means that only God has a hold of you. Your desires, your money, your destiny, your very life have been surrendered to God. It means you will only listen to God. It means you won't pick and choose what you'll obey, but will completely follow the instructions in his word.

To be soul'd out means you are crazy in love with God and crave Him more than anything else. It means you are a go-for-broke, all-in, no-holds-barred, full-speed-ahead follower of Jesus Christ. I say, "Amen all by myself!"

The most important decision you will ever make is to be soul'd out to Jesus. But it's not a decision God will force on you. It's your choice. You know the costs and you know the reasons for being soul'd out. Now, make a decision.

Become a Follower of Jesus

Have you placed your life in God's hands? Have you "stuck your toe" in His living water? If not, then what has a hold of you? You can receive Jesus' forgiveness and new life by saying "yes" to following Him. Below is a prayer you can pray to become a Christian—a follower of Christ—and receive His salvation.

"Heavenly Father, I admit that I have sinned and have not reached your standard. Today, I want to place my faith in Christ Jesus, your Son, who died on the cross and rose again to forgive my sins. I need and I want His life-changing power in my life. I surrender my will to you and accept your will for my life. Thank you for accepting me because of Christ. I look forward to a brand new life in Christ. I expect never to be the same, and I thank your for changing me. In Jesus name I pray, Amen."

If you Prayed the Prayer

If you just prayed that prayer, I want to be the first to say, "Welcome to the family of God!" You have just made the single most important decision you will ever make.

Please, don't keep this decision a secret. Phil and I would love to hear from you. Email us at: SouldOut@BOSSonline.org, and tell us about your decision so we can keep you in prayer. Also, be sure to tell a family member, a friend, or a pastor about your life-changing decision.

Finally, dive in! Find a friend, or a group of friends, to help you learn more about your new faith in Christ and help you build on this decision to be *Soul'd Out*. In fact, if you email us and tell us that you have prayed this prayer to become a Christian, Phil will send you a free study by Faith Alive 365 called *Start Strong* that you can use to get started.

Once you commit your life to following Christ, His resurrection power lives in you! Never forget that you have this incredible power source. Stay faithful, and it will empower you as you build rock-solid character and become a significant, *soul'd out* follower of Christ.

Decide to be Significant

"It's easy to make a buck. It's a lot tougher to make a difference."
-Tom Brokaw

Could you imagine a world without choices? Imagine going to a restaurant and never having a choice of what to eat. Day after day, it's always the same. Imagine never having a choice in the clothes you wear. Day after day, everyone wears the exact same thing. Imagine never having a choice in the work you do or the people you live with. You know what that kind of life is called? Prison.

We may sometimes be overwhelmed by the choices that confront us, but the reality is that we love to have choices. Marketers know this, and they cater to it.

When you buy a car, you get to choose from different makes, then models, then colors, and then customize it further with pricey options. When you go to the mall, you can shop at dozens of clothing stores that carry hundreds of styles. When you go to a coffee shop…you get the idea. No matter what you're looking for, there's always more than one choice—even if you want salt. It's crazy.

Choices are a part of life. We expect them. We demand them. Choices are what make life fun, interesting, and exciting. When we make choices we feel powerful and in control.

Choices can make our lives better, but they can also make things worse. The quality of your life will be determined by the quality of your choices. Follow my thinking here. Over the course of your life you will probably make billions of choices, and those choices will shape the quality of your life. But here's the amazing thing—in fact, this is the big point of this book. Out of billions of choices, there are really only a handful of key decisions that will determine the quality of your life. Those key decisions will determine whether you'll be a wonder or a blunder, whether you'll be significant or superfluous, whether you'll make a difference or just make a buck.

Out of billions of choices, there are really only a handful of key decisions that will determine the quality of your life.

These key decisions are crucial because they determine what kind of character you will have. And your character is important because it will determine how you make the billions of other choices you will face over your lifetime.

To live a life of significance, you need a rock solid foundation of character, and each decision I have shared with you in this book will help you develop that foundation.

- When you decide to be courageous, you won't let fear lead you to make bad choices.
- When you decide to avoid anger, you'll protect yourself, and those around you, from the damage anger can cause.
- When you decide to forgive, you will cure yourself of the poison of bitterness.
- When you decide to be content, you will be able to enjoy life rather than be consumed by it.
- When you decide to be generous, you will be in control of your resources of time, talent and treasure rather than allowing them to control you.
- And when you decide to serve, you will not only make the world better, you will protect yourself from the corrosive damage of pride.

These six decisions form the foundation of character, but the final decision is the cornerstone—it is the decision to be a go-for-broke, all-in, no-holds-barred, full-speed-ahead, soul'd out follower of Jesus Christ. This is the decision that fuels all the other decisions because it fills you with God's life. And once you experience God's life, you will settle for nothing less.

What does it mean to be soul'd out? It means you will be courageous, avoid anger, forgive, be content, be generous and serve God by serving those around you. To be soul'd out is to let God be the God of your life. You will follow Him exclusively and obey Him completely.

When you surrender yourself to God, you'll discover that God will give you a supernatural strength you never dreamed possible. You may never be a celebrity, but you will be a difference maker. You may never be important, but you will be significant.

The world doesn't need more celebrities or people with puffed-up self-importance. The world needs ordinary people like you and me who have the strength of character to be bold; who will bring peace where there is conflict; who will heal wounds by offering forgiveness; who will be models of contentment to an exhausted society; who will be generous rather than selfish; who will serve rather than demand; and who will be the light of Christ through soul'd out living. The world needs people who have substance, who make a difference, who are significant because they are godly. Will you decide to be that kind of person?

Although we live in a world of countless choices, only a few decisions will really matter. It's time you decide to be Soul'd Out!

Let us Hear from You

Our hope is that this book has helped encourage you to live a Soul'd Out life. If this book has been an encouragement to you, we'd love to hear about it. Let us know what God is doing in your life, the ways that you're seeking to be a soul'd out follower, and the difference that it's making. Please email us at SouldOut@BOSSonline.org, and share your story.

Study Questions
for Personal Reflection
or Group Study

Decide to take action! On the following pages are questions for each chapter that will help you engage with what you have been learning—and act on it. I encourage you to grab a few friends, work through these questions together, and allow God build your character so that it becomes rock-solid.

Chapter 1: Choices that Define You

- Do you want to be a person who is significant? Why?

- Do you think character is important? Explain.

- How would you describe godly character?

- Do you agree with Sherwood's belief that character building decisions are the most important decisions you'll ever make—even more important than decisions about who you will marry or what career you will choose? Give your reasons.

- On page 14, Sherwood offers seven life-changing decisions that he believes are crucial to developing rock-solid, godly character. Do you agree with Sherwood's choice of crucial decisions? Which of these seven decisions will be the most difficult for you to take action on?

- Read Matthew 24:12-13. Is Jesus speaking to people who believe in God, or don't believe in God? Is that significant? What does it mean that "the love of many will grow cold?" What would that look like?

- Gut-check time: Would you say that your own love for Jesus is growing warmer or colder? Why?

- Read Hebrews 11:24-28. Based on this passage, and anything else you can remember about Moses, what evidence is there that Moses was soul'd out to God? When you look at people today, what evidence do you look for that would suggest that they are soul'd out to God?

- Moses had no idea that God had big plans for him. How do you feel about the idea that God may have big plans for you that you might be unaware of? What will you need to do make yourself available to the plans God has for you?

PRAYER

If you're in a group, share one decision you are facing right now that you need wisdom to make. Then pray for the person on your right. Ask God to give them wisdom to make the decision they face, and ask God to work in their lives to build their character. If you're not in a group, pray the same things for yourself.

Chapter 2: Decide to be Courageous

- Vincent Van Gogh asked, "What would life be if we had no courage to attempt anything?" How would you answer that question?

- If you decide now to be courageous in any situation, how can that help you in the future to make good choices?

- Does it take courage to be soul'd out to Jesus? Explain.

- Read Joshua 1:1-9, 1 Samuel 17:32-37, 45-47, Psalm 23:4, Psalm 27, and Romans 8:31. Where can we draw our courage from?

- How do you develop a relationship with God that is exemplified in the above passages—the kind of relationship where you have no doubts that God is with you and has your back?

- What is one step you need to take in order to strengthen your relationship with God and become more conscious of His presence in your life? What has kept you from taking that step up until now?

- From the choices below, where do you need to have the most courage? Explain.

  a. At work

  b. With friends

  c. With family

  d. When you're alone

  e. Other

- Small acts of courage can lead to big acts of courage. From the list on page 38, which action would take the most courage from you? How can you act courageously in that area this week?

- Who do you know that needs en-*courage*-ment this week? How will you provide it?

PRAYER

If you've taken these questions seriously, you have made some decisions to act courageously as you draw upon your relationship with God. Now, pray for yourself and others in your group. Pray that you will have God's courage and strength to get off the fence and follow-through.

Chapter 3: Decide to Resist Anger

• When you walk into a room, are people more likely to take courage or take cover?

• Read Ephesians 4:26-27. When is anger healthy and when does it become harmful? What does it mean to "give the devil a foothold," and how can anger cause that to happen? Do you practice not letting the sun go down on your anger? Why or why not?

• Read out loud Psalm 34:11-14, Proverbs 12:20, Matthew 5:9, Romans 12:18, 2 Corinthians 13:11, Hebrews 12:14, and James 3:18. Do you think God might be trying to drive home a point? Why is this so important to God? How will this help us to avoid anger?

• What is the difference between being a peacemaker and a peace-keeper?

• James 3:6 describes the extensive damage our language can cause. Paraphrase in your own words what James means when he says that your tongue is a "world of evil among the parts of the body" (NIV), and that it "sets your life on fire." What kind of language will bring peace? How careful you are in your speech towards your family, friends, coworkers and strangers?

- Read Philippians 4:6-7. How can God's peace help us avoid anger? What do these verses teach us about what we can do to bring God's peace into our lives? How will these things help us avoid anger and experience peace?

- On pages 53-54, there is a list of steps you can take to resolve conflict and make peace. Which suggestion can help you the most? What else has helped you avoid anger?

- How can deciding to avoid anger be a benefit to your life? What practical steps will you take to start practicing this decision?

PRAYER

Practice the anger repelling prayer suggested in this chapter. Start by choosing an attribute of God that is meaningful to you, and praise God. For example, "God, I praise you for being a God of peace." Next, confess your tendency to get angry. If you can think of a recent incident of anger, confess that specifically. Then ask God to fill you with His peace and help you make peace-making responses when you start to feel angry. Also ask God to help you watch your tongue. Finally, give God thanks for specific ways you've been blessed recently. If you make this type of prayer a common practice, you will tap into God's power for avoiding anger and making peace.

Chapter 4: Decide to Forgive

- Why do we struggle to forgive people who have harmed us?

- Read Matthew 18:21-35. Why is forgiveness such a big deal to Jesus? What's at stake if we refuse to forgive someone? What does unforgiveness reveal about our relationship with Jesus?

- What does it mean to "forgive from the heart"? Reread the section on "A Recipe for Forgiveness," starting on page 66, if your need to refresh your memory.

- How is forgiveness beneficial to your life and your future?

- Who, if anyone, taught you how to forgive (not just that you should forgive)? What were you taught?

- Why is it important to identify the specific action you're forgiving? (see page 66)

- Why is it important to identify the feelings you felt as a result of that action? (see page 67)

- Why is it important to decide in advance to make forgiveness a "permanent attitude"? (see page 74)

- You don't have to share any details with your group unless you want to, but is there someone who comes to mind that you need to forgive? Can you take that step? What can help you?

PRAYER

Why not put the lessons of this chapter into practice right now? Use this prayer of forgiveness to "get off the hook," and allow God to heal past wounds and remove the poison of bitterness and anger.

Dear Jesus,

I choose to forgive (name of person), for doing (specific action that hurt you), and causing me to feel (the feelings you felt). Amen.

Chapter 5: Decide to be Content

- When you feel like your life is out of control, how do you react? Do you turn to comfort food, power shopping, watching hours of TV, plunging yourself into work, becoming snappy and more demanding, drinking, partying, or... what do you turn to?

- In this chapter, Sherwood suggests that we are never satisfied. Do you agree or disagree? Why?

- Read 1 John 2:15-17. What is being compared and contrasted in this passage? What does the passage say each offers? Which is said to offer something permanent? What is wrong with the cravings (or "lusts" in NIV) mentioned in this passage? Why does John consider them to be negative things?

- Read 1 Timothy 6:6-10. How does Paul's instructions compare to 1 John 2:15-17? What, if any, additional insight does Paul offer about our cravings and what we can do about them?

- Do you think contentment is beneficial? Would it improve the quality of your life? Would it help you make wiser choices? Explain.

- In this chapter, Sherwood taught that contentment is developed when we trust that God is in control and is for us (pages 84-89). Can we be certain that God is in control? Can we be certain that God is looking out for our best interests? Explain your reasons from your own experience and from scripture.

- How can our confidence in God's control, and our trust that He is for us, help us move from discontentment to contentment?

- Why doesn't contentment occur naturally? Why must we decide to be content?

- We don't always act, or react to unexpected situations, as if we believe God is in control. What is one specific thing you can do to develop more awareness and trust in God's control?

PRAYER

Start your prayer time by praising God and acknowledging His control over all of life. Confess any craving or discontentment you are experiencing that pulls you away from being soul'd out to Christ. Ask God to help you relax in His presence and trust in His plans for your life. Close by thanking God for specific ways he has blessed, protected and provided for you today.

Questions for Personal Reflection or Group Discussion

Chapter 6: Decide to be Generous

- When money is running tight in your household, how do you react? What are you like to be around? What emotions do you feel?

- Read Deuteronomy 8:11-18 and then Matthew 6:19-21, 24. According to these passages, what is the danger of money? What are we told to do to protect ourselves from this danger?

- Read 1 Timothy 6:9-10, and 6:17-19. Have your efforts to become wealthy, or your stress over finances, ever had a negative effect on your life? If you are willing, share examples with the group. What does Paul say we can do to "store up treasures in heaven?"

- How would you define generosity? How would you rate your own generosity on a scale of 1-10, with 10 being extravagantly generous and 1 being a Scrooge?

- Read Luke 16:10-11. What is the relationship between generosity and trust in God? What does our generosity or lack of generosity reveal, and what are the results?

172

- Read 2 Corinthians 9:6-15. List all the benefits and blessings mentioned in this passage that come as a result of generosity. What do these verses have to say to a person who says that they'd like to be generous, but cannot afford to be?

- How can the decision to be generous lead to a life of significance, and a failure to be generous lead to insignificance? Why must we decide to be generous?

- Do you need to be more generous? How will you do this? Towards whom will you be generous?

PRAYER

The following prayer is based on Psalm 119:36-37. Why not pray this out loud together.

"Dear Lord, we ask you to turn our hearts toward your statutes and not toward selfish gain. Turn our eyes away from worthless things, and provide for us as we follow your word and give generously."

Chapter 7: Decide to Serve

• Has pride ever gotten you into trouble? If you're willing, share a story.

• Read Matthew 23:1-12. How are the Pharisees described? Why does Jesus have a problem with them? Verses 11 and 12 summarize the point Jesus is making. In those verses, is Jesus making a suggestion, a demand, or a statement of fact? Have you ever tried to draw attention to yourself, make yourself look better than you really are, or "toot your own horn?"

• Read John 13:1-17. Note: Foot washing was always done by a servant. It was never done by the host or guests—they were too important. Yet Jesus washes the disciples feet. What's the not-so-subtle point Jesus is making?

• What is the value of serving?

• Where is God calling you to serve? Use the following questions to help you sense how God has "wired" you for service.

    a. What kinds of people catch your attention? What type of group are you most drawn to serve? For example: children, elderly, families, students, homeless, handicapped, immigrants, a specific nationality…you get the idea.

b. What area(s) of need do you care about? Do you love helping people with:

- Spiritual needs?
- Physical or health needs?
- Relational needs?
- Emotional needs?
- Educational needs?
- Vocational needs?
- Financial needs?

c. It is probable that the pull you feel towards certain people or needs reveals how God has "wired" you to serve. Based on your answers, can you think of an opportunity at your church, or in your community, where you can volunteer to serve and be used by God to make a difference in the areas you feel drawn towards? Share what that opportunity might be. If you cannot think of anything, ask the group for suggestions. Remember, nobody promised it would be convenient.

PRAYER

Pray that God will: open your eyes to see ways to serve, give you the courage to serve, empower your service, and allow you to be a "light of the world."

Chapters 8-9: Decide to be Soul'd Out

- People can be committed to many things—exercise, a sports team, a hobby, a club.... Name two activities you're committed to (not just what you participate in). What is the evidence of your commitment to these things? Would other people be able to observe and recognize your commitment?

- Sherwood believes we need "software" to run the first six character decisions. Why would that be true? Why wouldn't we be able to do these things on our own?

- How would you define a soul'd out follower of Christ? What would be the evidence of being soul'd out?

- Using the chapter eight's beach analogy for spiritual growth found on pages 135-137, do you see yourself as a toe dipper, wader, or kamikaze, or are you still on the beach?

- Read Luke 14:25-35. Do some brainstorming. Name as many costs to being soul'd out to Jesus as you can think of.

- Read Psalm 23, Psalm 37:4, Roman 6:23, John 10:10, Ephesians 3:14-19, Galatians 5:22-25. What are the benefits of being soul'd out to God that are mentioned in each passage?

- Read Psalm 95:1-7. What is the only reason to be soul'd out? Sherwood said that if we are not soul'd out, then we don't understand who God is. Do you agree? Explain.

- Read Luke 5:1-11. What would the catch of fish mean to professional fishermen? When the four fishermen decided to follow Jesus, they knew what they were leaving, but do you think they had any idea of what was ahead? Why would they leave everything? What would they have missed if they decided to stick with the haul of fish instead?

- A stumbling block to becoming soul'd out is that people know what they're leaving behind, but can't see what's ahead. They're afraid of the unknown. What about you? What are you focused on: what you're leaving behind or what is ahead?

You'll never actually know what's ahead until you decide to be a go-for-broke, all-in, no-holds-barred, full-speed-ahead follower of Jesus Christ. You'll never know what you're going to miss out on if you don't make that decision. But I promise you this, if you make the decision, you will be significant!

PRAYER

Tell God that you are choosing to be soul'd out, and ask Him for the strength to keep that commitment.

Questions for Personal Reflection or Group Discussion